COME
TO THE
TABLE
DIEM
BURDEN

DISCLAIMER

This story is based upon actual events and persons. I have tried to recreate events, locales and conversations from my memories of them. In order to maintain their anonymity in all instances, I have changed the names of individuals and places, except where written permission was given. I may have changed some identifying characteristics and details, such as physical properties, occupations and places of residence, as well as other descriptive details.

This book is dedicated to
The Shiny Club

Foreword

For my whole life – 55 years in total – I was a vocal atheist, with a fervent belief that the concept of an omniscient, omnipresent God, was just too preposterous to be real: the Bible was made up by power-hungry men during the demise of the Roman Empire; the need to believe in Jesus was indicative of some kind of personality weakness; the church was full of corrupt men doing bad things; and, seriously, what relevance did all of this ancient hocus-pocus have to do with a society in present-day life?

For me to give up that lifelong belief and become a follower of Jesus, nothing short of a miracle would be needed. Absolutely *nothing* would have made me believe in God. *Period.*

In 2021, following the sudden and unexpected death of my brother, I fell into a deep depression unlike anything I have ever felt before. My marriage came to an abrupt end after twenty years, and I was struggling to accept the loss of my brother.

I was down and lost, but I certainly wasn't looking for God – what would be the point in looking for something that didn't exist?

I was living in Spain and I'd met many people who were walking the pilgrimage route across the country – the *Camino de Santiago* – and many of *them* were asking questions, seeking answers to the purpose of life, seeking God, and just about everything else. They seemed more lost than me, and I was quite content to bumble along in my life of ignorance, with no desire to ask strangers absurd questions.

So what happened to me to make me change my mind? I can say this: it wasn't because I was *told* or *convinced* by somebody to have *faith*. It didn't happen because I was *brainwashed* by somebody – I'm too strong willed (stubborn even) to be swayed to believe in something that I was adamant did not, *could not*, exist. And it didn't happen because I was depressed and therefore vulnerable. In fact, you'll see that I was far from depressed when these extraordinary events happened to me.

I didn't become a *believer* in faith – somebody who accepted God based simply on faith, as many people do. That was not who I was. I stubbornly resisted what was happening to me, what I was being advised, what I felt, and what I was witnessing with my very own eyes – right until the hour that I couldn't deny it anymore. As the evidence rapidly built up against my lifelong belief, I withstood as long as I was physically and mentally able to. I hate being wrong, and to discover that I had been wrong *all* of my life? Impossible.

When I couldn't resist any longer, I didn't become just another *believer*, I became a *knower*. By this, I mean I met God personally. When this happened, I *knew* He existed, rather than just *believed* He did. *That* is what it would have taken, and that is precisely what happened.

My previous *belief* was atheism, and I gave it up after a few intense months. I now have a *conviction*, which is far stronger than a simple *belief*. I am convinced that Jesus was resurrected and lives to this day, because He is alive in me. Every single day, *I feel His presence*.

We can give up our beliefs based on fresh evidence, but a conviction is impossible to dismiss, as we'd have to lie to ourselves to justify it.

This story of how I found Jesus is well documented and corroborated. That this all happened in 2021 meant that technology recorded a lot of my message chats – which showed my state of mind – during this period. My story is supported by many contemporaneously written messages between me and those involved – all of whom have graciously given me permission to not only use these exchanges as written, but also to identify these wonderful individuals. This helped me considerably in recreating the events as accurately as possible.

I have also incorporated original texts written by me for no other reason than I am a writer and I love to write. I wrote these at the time of these events, and I use them raw – that is, unedited and genuine.

But one of the greatest sources of information I have had the good fortune of being able to access and use is the testimony of the many people involved in this story. Most of them keep daily journals, and have – most generously – given me access to their personal thoughts and observations written at the time, giving first-hand accounts of what they thought of me, and what they believed was happening, as it happened.

Recounting events by drawing on multiple sources helped to confirm that this wasn't just all in my head. This book is a retelling of that story: it explains why I gave up a 55-year belief in just three months, and accepted Jesus into my life.

My hope is that you, the reader, will not only enjoy this story but also find some answers amongst these words.

I'll finish this foreword with a quote that was given to me when I was midway through this story, which helped me to understand that even I was worthy of God's attention:

> *"I have been all things unholy; if God can work through me, He can work through anyone."*
> – Saint Francis of Assisi

CHAPTER 1

MONASTERY OF SANTA MARIÁ OF IRATXE, AYEGUI, NAVARRA

Wednesday 14 July 2021

I don't like churches. As a lifelong atheist, I was uneasy visiting *any* church, so I avoided going into them. Even at weddings and funerals, you'd find me hovering near the back door, ready to flee as soon as acceptable. The enormous doors were the only thing I liked about churches. You could always find the exit quickly.

We built these monumental structures with great wealth, whilst the poor died in the dirt outside. Unelected men (supposedly representing God), wearing expensive, heavily embroidered robes, dictating to the local population how they should behave (and perhaps even *think*?). And those ostentatious altars full of in-your-face bling? No thanks! Any visit always left a nasty taste in my mouth. Deep, entrenched distaste prevented me from visiting the Vatican with my two brothers – who felt the same as I did. It was just who we were.

This morning, however, I followed on behind my three new friends, who were leading me into a church in northern Spain. Perhaps I shouldn't have gone in, but I didn't want to be rude. I – an anti-church, uncompromising atheist – was entering a place of worship with three fervent believers, so I had to resist saying anything that might offend them.

This visit would change my life.

We were sightseeing on the *Camino de Santiago* (Way of St. James)

– the famous pilgrimage route across northern Spain. The church was attached to an abandoned monastery known as the *Monastery of Irache (Iratxe)*, near to *Estella* in *Navarra*. It has always been a must-see place whenever I have visitors, along with the nearby fountain, which dispenses free wine for passing pilgrims. I'd already seen it twice before, so my enthusiasm was low, although a free glass of wine wouldn't go amiss.

Monastery of Irache

Today, I was a guest of two people who were becoming my new friends: Wes and Sherry, a married couple from Canada. I'd bumped into them around our adopted Spanish village where they ran a café. We lived in

Viana, Navarra, a thirty-minute drive from the monastery.

I'd suspected that their café had a religious slant to it because they had a large wooden cross above the counter, and a sign on the back wall advertising 'Jesus Meditation' – whatever that was. They were warned that if there was any talk of Jesus, I would leave. It also confused me which religious group they belonged to, as they claimed they weren't 'religious'. I just shrugged my shoulders and kept my wits about me.

They'd invited me along for the visit, as they had a visitor staying with them from the United States. Kate was in her thirties and a volunteer at their café for three months. She'd only arrived two weeks earlier, and the Canadians were enjoying showing her the sights.

Kate had arrived in *Viana* on the 1st of July, and out of politeness I'd gone to the café to meet her on the 2nd. When told the new girl was in fact a *missionary*, I groaned. However, Kate was the opposite of any concept I had of a missionary, and by the third day we were best friends. That was just two weeks ago, and we'd met up every day since.

After this visit, we were to meet up with their friends who ran an *albergue* (a hostel for pilgrims). Their organisation had recently purchased a nearby abandoned monastery, and were refurbishing it, and making it into some kind of accommodation. We were going to have lunch with them next. I had an inkling that they were also 'religious', and I was worrying about how much Jesus-talk I'd be subjected to today. The word *sect* was also creeping into the back of my head.

After a brief visit to the free wine, we entered the vacant monastery, and – despite its being my third visit – I took yet more photos of the place. Kate had proven to be an excellent photographer and, as a result, I felt compelled to improve on my original pictures.

As we explored the building, we came to an ornate doorway. It led into a church. I would never have visited the church on previous visits.

I politely sidled in behind them.

The structure was beautiful. I love architecture, and the ceiling was just mesmerising. I walked around with my head tilted skywards, taking in the building's magnificence. As I walked, I took a lot of photos. After a full circuit of the entire floor, I walked it again such was its beauty.

The church interior, Monastery of Irache, Navarra

Looking upwards whilst walking was making me dizzy – or was it the beauty of the ceiling that was responsible? Whatever it was, it was becoming uncomfortable, so I focused on what was in front of me, to help the feeling pass. I wandered towards the front of the church to rummage around at the 'business end'.

The building was devoid of all the usual trappings of church wealth – all the typical, ostentatious, gold and shiny stuff. In fact, it was quite stunning in its simplicity and elegance.

I walked up to the raised platform at the end. The altar had a white linen cloth draped over it – the church was still in use, although the monastery had been long-abandoned. To one side was a small glass cabinet containing something of interest. I walked over, bent down, and read the hand-painted text on the front of it: *Reliquias de S. Veremundo (8)* (Relics of Saint Veremundo, number 8).

Right up my street! I didn't know who Saint Veremundo was, but I loved history and relics.

The case contained a white satin cushion with elegant gold embroidery (I knew there'd be gold somewhere). Sat atop the cushion was a mummified finger, wrapped in (more) gold thread with a purple seal attached to the thread. I felt uncomfortable that it might indeed be the poor old fella's finger I was gawping at. Many relics in churches were body parts of dead saints, and I wondered if they'd be happy about this if they knew?

And then I swooned. It was that feeling again. I stood upright, grasped the corner of the relic stand, and focused. Was this dizziness? Was it what happened when I was looking up at the ceiling?

No, it wasn't. This was something new for me. Centred in my chest, it was more like an emotion – though unlike any I'd ever experienced. And, more worryingly, it was increasing in intensity.

I thought of my younger brother who'd had a heart attack two years ago. Was this happening to me? Was this the first symptom? I walked around the altar and back towards my friends, as I was very vulnerable. I needed to hold on to something – to somebody.

As the expanse of the cavernous church came into my view again, I became shaky on my feet. So this was it? Was I – a lifelong atheist – having a heart attack in the presence of three believers in God? I was about to die, and in *a bloody church*! My brothers would find the circumstances of my demise hilarious.

And then an angelic voice – a female – singing praise to God in that monumental space. It echoed around the rafters above my head – the acoustics perfectly formed just for her voice. I looked up. Had I been wrong all my life? Was there an angel singing, or a staircase descending?

Nothing.

The tiny figure stood at the far end of the church, her hand resting on the side of a pew. She was facing skywards and singing with a voice that shouldn't have come from someone so small.

Sherry – of course. She would do something like that, although I didn't know she sang so well. I looked around and saw Kate watching her too. I looked at my feet and realised I was still standing, still alive, but the surging in my chest continued. Had I been in a bar, I might have suspected my drink had been spiked. The sensation, so new and so overpowering, rendered me speechless. *What was happening to me?*

Sherry's song ended, and the others asked her to do it again as they lifted their mobile phones. I fumbled with mine, and recorded some of her singing too. I later learned of The Doxology:

> *"Praise God from whom all blessings flow; Praise Him, all creatures here below; Praise Him above ye heavenly host; Praise Father, Son, and Holy Ghost."* – Thomas Ken (1637 - 1711)

I stood motionless. What would happen next? Could I even walk?

The three of them exited the church, talking excitedly about Sherry's singing ability, oblivious to the subdued atheist, plodding on behind them, pondering his fragile mortality with renewed fear. I followed them to the car and quietly got in the back. The trio were still animated. I just sat there – in silence – as they drove the ten-minute trip to their friends' monastery.

That unique, overwhelming surge, which first appeared there – the very minute before Sherry sang her praise – has remained with me since. Sometimes so strong, it takes my breath away, and I have to grab onto something to steady myself.

Another three weeks passed before I discovered what 'it' was.

CHAPTER 2

EIGHT MONTHS EARLIER

Thursday 8 October 2020

It was just a week before my mum was to celebrate her 80th birthday. "I've got cancer."

It's a phrase nobody wants to hear from a loved one. It brings nothing but fear, heartache, and the dread of the awful unknown.

My father had died of a heart attack twenty-five years earlier, leaving behind our mum and her sons. Except for me, they all lived in or near our home town of Uttoxeter, a small market town just north of Birmingham, England. The family now comprised our mum and her five sons: Paul, Michael, me, Peter, and Richard – in this order. Mum lived alone in the family home.

Paul (58 years). Single, a trucker, ex-airborne soldier, and the strongest of the five of us.

Michael (57 years). Married, just retired from the police service, and looking forward to a new life of leisure.

Then me (55 years). Married, living in Spain for the past twenty years.

Peter (54 years), my younger brother, registered disabled and dependent on a mobility scooter. Divorced, living with Paul who helped him to get around. Peter had suffered a heart attack the previous year.

The youngest, Richard (50 years). Diabetic, lived with his long-term girlfriend and worked away from home.

It was Mick speaking to me on the phone. He'd come to Spain last year, and we'd met up for lunch and spent a lovely day together at the beach in *San Sebastian*. Unbeknown to me, he'd discovered a lump on his neck whilst there, which had just been diagnosed as cancer of the throat.

He wouldn't know the prognosis until after more scans, but we knew throat cancer had taken our mum's sister. We dreaded what was to come.

Two days later, Mick created a *WhatsApp* group for family and friends, so that he could post updates of his battle with the illness. On the run-up to mum's birthday, the messages were full of humour, family banter, positivity, and progress reports.

Paul, the main lynchpin of the family, took mum and the others out to celebrate her eightieth birthday, even though he was suffering himself from 'Long Covid' symptoms. His cough was back, and he was losing weight, and doctors were experimenting with different treatments for him.

I knew Paul well – he was the toughest man I had ever met – so I wasn't worried about him. Mick was our principal concern.

Sunday 25 October 2020

Five days after mum's birthday, Paul was admitted to hospital 'for tests'. We created another *WhatsApp* group for his updates. I contacted him and asked if there was anything I could do for him. Over the next few days, his messages made less and less sense to us. It was clear he was trying to communicate, but it was quite garbled and often nonsensical, and we were worried about why.

Thursday 29 October 2020

Four days later, Mick phoned me to say that Paul didn't have 'Long Covid' after all. What he had was far, far worse – it was lung cancer. Just twenty-one days had passed since Mick had been diagnosed with cancer. Now Paul had cancer too.

I messaged Paul. His response wasn't clear, but he told me it "wasn't gonna be good!!!!" After a few back-and-forth messages, I feared the worst, and asked him if he was telling me I would not see him again.

"It's big! Doctors don't look positive."

I felt the dread creeping into my heart, but I reassured him they could perform miracles these days.

Over the next week, Paul's *WhatsApp* group grew in number as extended family and friends heard the news and joined it. People told us they were praying for him, and us. The brothers pulled together and became closer than we have ever been, and we all rallied around mum.

The family was struggling with this. Paul was mum's first born. Mick had grown up closest in age to him, and was dealing with his own cancer treatment and fears. Pete was suddenly without his housemate and lifeline to the outside world. Paul, the eldest, was a hero to Rich, the youngest. I lived far away, and therefore rarely saw them. This was also the time of Covid.

Information was shared regarding Paul's treatment and progress, and hopes raised, and then dashed, with each passing day.

I discovered Paul had finally found love, and I felt guilty that I didn't know. Why was I living in Spain? My family needed me, but the UK was back in full lockdown. Even travelling was out of the question.

Our big brother seemed to respond better to his treatment as October became November, although nobody could visit him for fear of bringing Covid onto the ward. There was even talk of him coming home soon, if he continued to improve.

Thursday 5 November 2020

Today we received an informative update. Paul's cancer was very advanced, and a side effect was a build-up of calcium in the blood, which leads to confusion. This was fluctuating, so some days Paul seemed better than others. Paul had ordered no visitors, and was withdrawing into himself, although on this day, Peter forced the issue, and they chatted together for an hour with his doctor. The doctor confirmed that the cancer was in one lung, but had spread to his surrounding bones. It was stage four and therefore incurable. Paul needed to face aggressive chemo to give him more time, but the problem was his lack of weight – he needed to put weight on before they could start treatment, but he wasn't eating. If they could increase his body weight, he might face the treatment and survive for a while longer, though how much longer was anybody's guess. The present goal was to stabilise the calcium level to keep him lucid and bring back his appetite.

Thursday 12 November 2020

Two and a half weeks after Paul went into the hospital, Mick began his radiation treatment.

At 3.30pm that day, Paul sent me a message: "*Hmm, Covid.*"

He had contracted Covid whilst in the hospital.

That was the last thing he needed! Covid *and* lung cancer? My worries surged. I feared that he wouldn't survive this combination. He was put onto High Flow Oxygen and moved to a respiratory ward.

Through tears, I wrote to him constantly and sent him voice messages, not knowing if he was reading anything from anybody.

Friday 13 November 2020

Me: "I hear you are on the happy juice today? Bet you feel like Superman right now???? I miss you, Paul. You've always looked after me, much more than I've deserved. I was never without beer money when you were around, and I wanna thank you for that. It's great that I can now return the favour, like the last time you came here, and next time you won't have to spend a penny! We'll eat great food, get slaughtered, and watch TV all night long, and do some metal-detecting in my enormous garden, which is just a few hundred metres from the village wall. You are the best kind of big brother: mega-generous, in money and in deed (just like dad was), and hard as nails. I'm sure you are fighting hard right now and giving it your all. Don't give up, Paul. There are so many people rooting for you right now. We want you back. X."

Later that day: "I fell in love with rock music when I was about 8 or 9 years old. I'd come home from school and hear 'Bat Out of Hell' blasting out of the box room bedroom on your record player, the one with the single speaker in the lid. Remember that? You later gave me the LP, and it was wafer thin. Ever since, rock has brought me such pleasure in life, and it was all thanks to you…"

I played *Meatloaf's Bat Out of Hell* album all night that night and got emotional and drunk. My heart was breaking. Saturday passed in a haze. On Sunday, I recovered somewhat. I decided it was time for me to get some exercise, to look after myself better. I was the only brother with no long-term serious medical condition, and I was taking my health for granted.

Sunday 15 November 2020, 12.11pm

Me: "Hi Paul, hope you feel OK today? I'm fine. Bit lost at the mo with not having a job, so to speak. This retirement thing means you have to be really disciplined to do things or you can easily stagnate. Not really into writing much, can't get in the mood for it with all that's going on back home! So eat some food, get home, and get well enough to receive treatment. We're all counting on you! I'm trying to motivate myself to go for a run today, the first one in years!!!"

I got myself ready to do just that – something I hadn't done in decades. I changed and began warming up, stretching on the patio. As I was doing this, my younger brother Peter called me.

"Paul has just days to live."

It was the first confirmation that there wasn't hope. I would never see my big brother again. He would never come and visit me in Spain again. He'd never take me metal-detecting again. It floored me. It broke me. I told my wife the news and ran.

I ran for about eight kilometres up in the hills around my home. I ran, and I cried, and I screamed, and I shouted aloud – and I cursed a God I didn't believe in for doing this to such a decent man. It was just so unfair.

I got home exhausted, and collapsed on the sofa, full of pain and hurt. Then the phone rang again: it was Rich, my youngest brother.

"I don't know how to tell you this, so I'm just going to say it: Paul just died…"

❖

Paul had died whilst I was out running. Throughout my life, he had been there for me. He had given me most of the things that give me pleasure in my life: rock music, craft beer, a love of travel, of fitness, and of motorbikes. He was the greatest of protectors, the most generous of people, and he was gone – all alone – at 58.

I didn't know at the time that his last words to me would be "*Hmm, Covid*". It could have been something more personal, but Paul wasn't like that. I'm just so glad that he died quickly, and he didn't suffer the indignity of a long, drawn-out death. He didn't deserve that, and he wouldn't have wanted all the fuss of such a death.

Later that night, I posted the following message on Paul's Progress group:

> *"You can't choose family, and some people get lucky, whilst others don't. I got lucky. Paul, my eldest brother, looked out for his four younger brothers in so many ways. He was rock hard, fearless, and genuine. All the attributes the eldest brother should have, and he had them in abundance. But his greatest asset was his generosity. Like our father, he was the most generous person you could wish to know. Generosity was in his heart, it was in his soul, it was what made him. Four weeks ago, despite being seriously ill, he drove our mum to Burton to buy her 80th birthday present. Today, he left us. Five became four. He was the first of us to arrive, and the first of us to leave. He was a guy I deeply admired, somebody I wanted to emulate in so many ways. He gave me my love of rock music and introduced me to metal-detecting. We drove for 24 hours in a car to Rome together and then back again. We did so much in the short time he had on this earth. I wished we'd done more together, much more. Tonight, he drinks in Valhalla with our dad, and boy will there be some sore heads tomorrow. From one soldier to another, I salute you, Paul. I love you and miss you like you wouldn't believe.*
>
> *Rest In Peace my brother and friend. May we meet again. X."*

Paul James Burden (1962 - 2020)

CHAPTER 3

THE FUNERAL

December 2020

Richard and Peter, my two younger brothers, took the lead. There was a lot to organise, including collecting Paul's possessions, which was very hard for them. They organised the whole funeral, as our mum was not really in position to do so, and our eldest, Mick, was receiving his treatment for cancer, and trying to get his head around that, whilst dealing with his own shock and grief.

I was desperate for a date so that I could book a flight, go into hotel quarantine, and be there for the funeral. Everything was up in the air with international travel because of damned Covid, but I had to be there.

Richard and I volunteered to read a tribute, which we were honoured to do. We wrote our speeches and read them out to each other over the internet, but neither of us could make it to the end. We were unsure if we could get through them at the funeral.

We finally set the funeral for 10.30am on Monday the 7th of December. It was to be a minor affair, limited to a maximum of thirty people and thirty minutes at Stafford Crematorium. The last time I was there was to bury our father.

When I booked the only flight I could find, via Amsterdam to Birmingham, there were only four seats taken. It was my absolute belief that people were not travelling in times of Covid, and that my flight would ultimately be cancelled, and I'd end up missing the funeral.

Sunday 6 December 2020

The flight was to go ahead. I left my Spanish home at 1.00am and drove through the night to Madrid airport. I checked in with my wheeled hand luggage at 4.30am, and boarded the flight to Amsterdam at 6.00am. Covid restrictions were in full force, and everybody was required to wear a mask as soon as they entered the airport and throughout the flight.

The plane was totally packed, and there were no gaps between me and the unknown people on either side of me. We were all elbow friendly.

Once the plane got airborne, coffee and sandwiches were brought round by the cabin crew, and everybody – and I mean *everybody* – calmly removed their masks and ate and drank simultaneously, whilst sitting almost on top of each other.

I was en route to see my 80-year-old mother, along with my brother who was undergoing chemotherapy. I *would not* remove my mask for a coffee on a three-hour flight to Amsterdam, and risk taking Covid to them.

Whilst everybody else indulged in coffee and Covid, I checked my ticket and procedures for once we landed in Amsterdam. I was surprised to see that I had just twenty minutes to catch my connection to Birmingham. *Twenty minutes?* If I missed the flight, I'd have to go on the flight the following day, and I'd miss the funeral. I asked a cabin crew member about the distance between the gates at the terminal, stating it was of the utmost importance that I make the connection. Maybe I might be let off first to facilitate the transfer?

She asked me why and I told her. Instantly sympathetic – especially as most people were going home to celebrate Christmas with their families – she said she'd ask the captain for me, as he knew the airport.

Just before we landed, the captain came to me with an Amsterdam airport guide. He'd marked the gate we were to land at, the gate I needed to be at, along with the route to get there. He said I should make it okay if I ran, and if passport control was not busy.

Thank you, KLM. You were amazing!

I ran all the way to passport control. There were just two staff on duty, and two long queues of people. I watched to identify which of the two staff members was the more efficient, but it was neither of them. There must have been fifty people in each queue, and there was little movement. I joined the one that seemed the shortest, and after ten minutes I realised we hadn't moved at all, yet the other queue had. So, I crossed the barriers and joined the other queue. As soon as I had done so, the other queue filled up with a fresh planeload of people, meaning I couldn't rejoin that one. Then a third police officer appeared on the scene, opened up a booth, and started checking passports in that queue.

The queue I'd just left was now being filtered towards two desks, and began moving at twice the speed of the queue I was in. My queue was still waiting on the progress of the lady at the single window, who clearly hated her job. Or people. Or both.

By the time I got through, I'd missed my connection to Birmingham. After I scowled at the officer and legged it, I followed the dotted line kindly marked on the map by the captain. I ran up to the desk in a panic.

"This is important to me. Please let me through. Please!"

The lady at the desk was trying to tell me something as I begged and pleaded with her.

Eventually, I understood and turned around. The flight was delayed, and all the passengers were sitting at the gate, quietly waiting, watching me and my performance.

I smiled and sat down in relief.

The hour and fifteen-minute flight to Birmingham eventually left at 9.45am, and the coffee fiasco was repeated once again.

I landed at 11.00am, and Richard came to pick me up. He stopped at the curbside and got out of his car. We embraced because we were too numb to say anything. We got in the car and I realised I was still wearing my mask, as was Richard. Under the circumstances, we were required to wear them by law. I had been wearing mine since I'd arrived at Madrid airport at 4.30am. I hadn't taken it off in six and a half hours.

At about 11.45am, he dropped me off at my hotel for my quarantine – I couldn't even see my hurting mum and give her a hug. Pulling my hand luggage behind me, I watched as Richard drove off, then I entered the hotel. I so needed to remove that damned mask – and sleep.

My hotel was on the outskirts of my home town of Uttoxeter, in the

Midlands. It was at a small truck stop area just off the A50 bypass, and it looked nice online.

I was told by a receptionist to leave the hotel 'because of Covid', and my room wouldn't be ready until about 1.00pm. I asked if I could leave my bag in reception, and again I was told it wasn't possible 'because of Covid'.

I told the lady that I was extremely tired and stressed, and that I'd been travelling for about eleven hours, that I hadn't slept at all since Friday night, and that the reason I was here was because of Covid. That it was bloody Covid that had finally taken my brother, and that I was here for his funeral. I was angry and desperate.

Her tone softened slightly, and she explained they were extremely short-staffed and that I could have called in advance to book an early check-in. I told her I had called yesterday about a *dozen* times, and that nobody had answered the phone. She pointed out that they were short-staffed because of Covid, and that I could wait in the rest area of the Starbucks Café if I wanted to be more comfortable.

Deciding that there was no point in arguing, and that a Gingerbread Latte and a Roast Turkey & Stuffing sandwich were actually highly desirable, I decided to head across to Starbucks and take a seat there, to eat a slow brunch along with my wheeled suitcase, and maybe read a UK newspaper in the warm, whilst waiting for my room to be readied.

"Sorry, love. You can't sit inside the café – *Covid!*" She nodded at the customers queuing up at the drive-through window, as if in admonishment. *Should have stayed in your car, duh…*

"So, where can I eat my delicious Christmas sandwich and drink my festive drink then?"

"You'll have to eat it outside."

"But I don't see any seats outside. Is there anywhere to sit outside? *And… it's raining now…*"

"Sorry, nothing I can do about it. It's–"

"Yeah, I know – Covid."

I stood there like a fool, trying to balance my large Gingerbread

Latte in one hand without burning my fingers, and the dripping toasted sandwich in the other, whilst balancing my luggage handle against my thigh.

"Look," she said, suddenly remembering her humanity. "There's a smokers' corner just around there. There aren't any seats, but there is a bit of a roof to shelter you from the rain."

I thanked her and followed her pointy finger.

There was a small area for smokers to indulge in their delightful habit, along with a tiny overhang to protect me. It had no tables, no seating, no shelves, no anything – just bins over-filled with stubbed-out, stinking cigarette butts, and a floor carpet of the same.

Both of my hands were full. The sandwich was too big and hot to consume one-handed, as was the extra-large drink. I had to put one of them down to use both hands on the other. The only option was the filthy floor, so I placed my drink down and focused on devouring my sandwich.

I stood and ate, taking in the area beyond the disgusting smokers' corner. The cafe was tucked away in the far corner of the service area. Their drive-through lane passed across the front of the smokers' corner, and was extremely busy, seeing as nobody could enter the café. A queue of cars formed a line just a few metres away from me. The car occupants had nothing to do, and nothing to see except for me. For the next hour, I became the centre of attention for every car-driving customer of that café, along with all of their partners and kids. *Who was this pathetic-looking creature in that stinking place, with a suitcase, taking an inordinate amount of time drinking his Christmassy Gingerbread Latte?*

After an hour of dragging out the latte, I realised two things: I had finished the drink, and I was freezing. Simply being sheltered from the freezing rain wasn't good enough – I'd been living in Spain for the past twenty years, and now I was standing for over an hour in Stink Corner, in a typical British December wind, while the world crawled by and stared at me from the comfort of fully heated Range Rovers and Audi 4x4s, their kids playing *I Spy with My Little Eye, Something Beginning with I…*

"Idiot!"

"Correct!"

Time to head to the hotel and refuse to move, regardless of Covid. What really added to the misery was the fact there was no clear footpath between the café and the hotel. It was as if only cars were welcome, and pedestrians had no place there. I had to drag my suitcase between terrifyingly large articulated lorries that were parked up for the night. I trudged along muddy tracks across unloved border lawns – the trampled mud clearly showing where a footpath needed to be laid – and finally arrived back at the hotel. It only took about five minutes, but I felt like I had just passed an army selection test.

The automatic swing door made me jump, and I entered reception fully prepared for a fight.

"Your room is ready for you now, Sir. Sorry for the delay. It's because of Covid…"

"Yeah, I know. I understand. Not much we can do about it, I suppose? What are the opening times for the restaurant, please?"

"Er, it's not open, because of…" She stopped when she saw my face.

"So, I have to quarantine here for *five* days, and I'm not allowed to *leave* the hotel for anything except my brother's funeral, and your restaurant is *closed*. What am I supposed to eat, then?"

She told me I had to order in, and they'd bring the food up to my room for me. I thought about it and smiled. Tonight: Fish and Chips. Tomorrow night: Curry Night. Tuesday night: Crispy Peking Duck. Wednesday, back to Spain, and tortilla.

I checked in, found my room, and closed the door. For the first time in my life, I was a stranger in my home town. An unwelcome outcast, forced to hole up in a small hotel with no room service. My family was one member less, and I had to quarantine.

Reality was collapsing in all around me.

I fell onto the bed and realised I still had my mask on. It was 1.00pm. Except for my garden lunch, the mask had been on my face for seven and a half hours, and it hurt like hell.

I ripped it off and threw it in the corner.

I showered, ate fish and chips, practiced my tribute speech, and slept like a baby.

Monday 7 December 2020

I took in some fresh air by walking up to my family's home, and stood on the pavement in front of my mother's house. I waved at her and she at me – like old neighbours – through her lounge window.

A number of people came to pay their respects, with everybody maintaining a safe distance. It was difficult for me to recognise most people, as they had aged since I'd last seen them, and they were wearing masks. They probably didn't recognise me either, standing there all alone.

At the appointed time, the hearse approached the house. Walking in front was an extremely tall undertaker dressed all in black, followed by two more walking behind the vehicle. They stopped outside the family home. Paul's coffin was proudly draped with his maroon beret and belt from his military service in the Parachute Regiment.

As my family, all from the same 'bubble', jumped into the limo, I jumped alone into a taxi and followed the convoy to the crematorium. Once there, Richard and I helped carry Paul into the building. Peter followed, as did Mick, but having to keep a distance from everybody.

We took our seats, and the brief service began. I sat alone.

Photos of Paul were being shown on a large screen. I smiled when an accidental photo of Paul's tiny caravan came up – one he used for his weekends away. *How did that get in there?*

Richard read his tribute first and got through it without falling apart. Then it was my turn.

My tribute to our brother, Paul:

"Love is not a word that Paul was entirely comfortable with. I certainly would never have told him I loved him, nor did I ever expect to hear it from him. Even hugging was avoided at all costs, unless you happened to be an attractive woman, that is.

But everybody who knew Paul loved him – it was hard not to: he was

27

as hard as nails, and as strong as an ox, yet in truth, he was the most gentle, caring, and selfless man you could ever wish to meet.

Paul demonstrated his love, not in words, but in deeds.

One freezing December morning, for example, he took me metal-detecting, to introduce me to his passion. Frustrated at finding nothing but ring-pulls and rusty old nails, after about ninety minutes I was well and truly ready to call it a day. Paul sensed this, and he quietly dropped a coin he'd found earlier, and nonchalantly smothered it in grass and soil with his foot.

"Dave, try over here…" he said.

Paul would rather have given up a precious, unidentified coin than to see me frustrated or failing.

Many years ago, when my wife Paula first met my family, she asked me:

"Dave, why does Paul always take the mickey [tease or ridicule in a friendly way] out of me? Doesn't he like me or something?"

"If he's taking the mickey out of you," I replied. "It's because he loves you."

Paul was my eldest brother, and Paul was the epitome of what an older brother should be, in so many ways:

First, he was my friend. Wherever he was in the world – and he certainly travelled – I knew I had a friend I could depend on, out there somewhere, and his friendship to me was a bond of blood, which no silly argument can break (and we did have our arguments).

Paul was fearless. Boy, was he fearless… In any fight, he'd not just be there for you, but actually in front of you, fighting for you. Paul feared nothing, and he feared nobody, as his front teeth will testify to. And he was certainly the kind of guy you wanted to have on your side in a fight.

Paul was dependable. In the dull routine of day-to-day life, he'd always be there for you, for me, for anybody and everybody, but none more so than for Pete, and for our mum.

Generous to a fault, he'd always be the first to put his hand in his pocket, to offer to drive you somewhere or pick you up, regardless of the time or distance. Whatever you needed, whenever you needed it, you knew Paul would be there for you.

Paul was all of this (and more besides) because he was inherently a good person, with a massive heart. He loved his family and friends, and we all loved him back in return – even if we didn't say it to his face.

Paul, to say I am proud of you is an understatement. You taught me so much about life, and you gave me so much to appreciate in life. I even thank you for giving me that smack once, one I fully deserved, I know! It was a wake-up call from a man I truly admired and respected, and it did the trick. I'm not sure who was more surprised by your punch: me, you, or poor old dad sitting in the front passenger seat.

Paul, if I asked you to name your greatest achievement in life, you'd probably say it was passing P Company [the selection and training course for the Parachute Regiment], and few would argue with that. I know that you nearly died trying, such was your determination to become a Para.

But you achieved far more than that, Paul – far, far more. You became the son that your mum and dad had hoped you'd become. You set a high standard for your brothers to try and emulate. And you became a friend to all who met you.

Your legacy, Paul, is found not in your maroon beret, not in any lucky find in a muddy field, nor will it ever be written down in any book (or maybe it will…).

Your legacy is clear for all to see, Paul. It can be seen in each of your brothers: in Mick, in Pete, in Rich, and in me, for without you as our big brother, we'd be half the men we have become.

We are what we are today, Paul, because of who you were before us.

When I first heard you'd been admitted to hospital, I wasn't unduly concerned. But after a few days, it became apparent just how serious your situation was. Each day seemed to bring more bad news as the short weeks passed by, and I began to prepare myself for the unthinkable. I sent you a spoken message every morning and evening, sometimes more. These messages contained words of encouragement, of support, some of humour even. Basically, good old brotherly banter. Occasionally, they were the rambling words of a drunken brother, slowly falling apart.

I'll never know if you heard my words, Paul, but it gives me great comfort believing that you must have. But there was one thing I never said to you, in any of those messages, or at anytime in our lives, so I'll say it to you now.

I love you, Paul, and have always loved you, and I can say that to you now, knowing that you won't feel awkward for it. Thank you for always being there for me.

I'd like to finish with a small poem:

You only hurt when you live
For you now, there is no pain
It's something I'll carry with me
Until we meet again
And when once more I find you
You'll hear me not complain
Of my loved ones left hurting
Standing in the rain
Life for me continues
With tears, I cannot contain
You only hurt when you live
Now nothing, will be, the same.

Thank you."

"You only hurt when you live"
© 2020 Diem Burden

CHAPTER 4

POST FUNERAL

Once the cremation was over, we all filed out into the carpark. There was nowhere else to go. Many people were hugging, but many people couldn't hug because of Covid or the dangers of Covid. I met some friends and relatives I hadn't seen in years, and I was numb.

There was no wake – something Paul would have wanted us all to have. Mum asked a few back to her house, including me of course. I just wanted to hug her, but I wasn't supposed to, nor was I allowed to go to her house. But I couldn't *not* go.

I went back there alone, by taxi, just as I had arrived, and, once inside, I hugged her. We had no choice. As for Mick, we all had to keep our distance as he was immunocompromised due to his ongoing treatment, and he couldn't come to the family home.

That night I went back to my hotel room and ate my favourite Indian meal alone.

Tuesday 8 December 2020

I met Pete and Rich at Pete's house for a drink together. It was the first time I had stepped inside his house without Paul being present. Paul was everywhere – his boots were still by the back door, his coats on the hooks. Even his metal detector was visible, protruding out of a field bag, a small light still flickering, showing it hadn't been turned off. It was as if Paul was still there.

It was tough, very tough for me. How Peter managed, I'll never know.

Wednesday 9 December 2020

I boarded the flight back to Spain, numb with grief and totally at a loss as to what had just happened. Michael still didn't know how his illness would end, and he was undergoing some awful treatment meanwhile.

As I flew away, I reflected on the dreadful year that was 2020. It was the worst year of my life and, as we were now in December, it was almost over. I hated to think of how Christmas would be for my mum and brothers in the next few weeks, but I was just so glad to see the end of 2020. With just three weeks left of the year, I was sure that nothing else could make the year any worse than it already had been. *Nothing…*

Once back home, I took comfort in my three dogs. Their love is always so unending, and without judgment.

My home life was tough. My wife of twenty years and I should have separated long ago, but we shared a business and a home, and roots run deep. Nathalia, her 20-year-old niece from Brazil, also lived with us, and we'd all suffered a terrible three-month lockdown in our house together, although we were fortunate in that it was a large house with an immense garden.

Saturday 12 December 2020

It had been almost four weeks since Paul had died, and just five days since his cremation. I drank a fair amount of alcohol that night. My niece, Nath (pronounced *Natch*), was having an online party, and she drank a considerable amount too.

We were re-enacting a fight scene we had just seen on TV, one that I believed she'd be able to escape from, following the moves I'd taught her in lockdown. I hadn't realised how drunk she was until she kicked me in the balls. It was effective, and allowed her to escape my hold, though it wasn't a move I'd taught her, nor had expected her to use on me!

I told her to focus, and to try again, and she did, this time punching me in the jaw. I couldn't stop laughing at her effective and surprising defensive moves, and quietly held her in high regard.

Then my wife came downstairs and demanded to know what was happening. It was an ongoing issue, one that I declined to be drawn into, so I just ignored her. She blocked the lounge door so that I couldn't just walk away, and this led to some pushing and shoving, which made her even angrier. And then, probably more out of frustration than anything, she called the police.

As we waited, I reminded her of the quantity of domestic abuse incidents that happen in Spain every day, and how the police were required to take positive action, usually against the man. She called them back and cancelled, but, of course, they couldn't cancel. They had to attend.

The *Guardia Civil* [The Civil Guard – a para-military police force in Spain] duly arrived. They spoke to her, then to Nath, and then to me. My wife told them she had cancelled them and that there was no complaint, but the officer arrested me anyway and took me to her patrol car, despite my perfectly reasonable behaviour and lack of any complaint from my wife.

Military Police. They are soldiers. They follow orders. They don't have any powers of discretion, and that is why, speaking as an ex-UK police officer, I can truthfully say that policing a *civilian* population with *military* personnel is just plain wrong. It does not work. It *cannot* work.

To be marched off like that was awful, but what happened to me next was, without a doubt, the most humiliating experience of my life.

Tuesday 15 December 2020

I wrote this down on the day after they released me, whilst the trauma of the experience was still fresh in my mind:

"The first shame came when the two large patrol cars drove up to the house with blue lights on, and they put me into the back of one of them. I'm sure the nosy neighbour was enjoying the spectacle.

They took me to the local Guardia Civil station, and sat me in the office whilst taking down my details and putting them into the computer, and fumbling around, trying to print out my rights in English. I'd told them I would make no comment, and wanted all forms in English.

This took about thirty to forty minutes. They treated me well and eventually gave me a copy of my rights. I declined a lawyer, so one was appointed for me, anyway. Eventually I asked to go to the loo, and was allowed to take a pee whilst being watched by an officer. When I returned, a lawyer was there for me, and we had a private chat. It became clear at this point that I would not be going home tonight.

They then asked me to spread, and they searched me, removing all of my personal effects and putting them in a bag, except for my watch, which they missed. They then took some fingerprints from me using ink and paper.

I was told they would transfer me to a holding area and that I'd be taken in front of a judge on Sunday, or, if not possible, on Monday. It was now obvious that I would probably be in custody all of Sunday and into Monday. I was confused, as my wife had cancelled the police from attending prior to their arrival, and my lawyer had told me she had no marks on her body to support her initial allegation. What was I being held for? I know the police have to attend all reports of alleged domestic violence and take action (usually against the man), but this seemed excessive – out of control, even.

After about ninety minutes, two more officers arrived to take me away. They handcuffed me to my front. Usually, I was the one putting handcuffs on nasty, violent criminals. Now, it was happening to me, despite my perfectly decent behaviour the entire time.

"It's for your protection," the cop said. "But I don't need protecting from myself," I thought.

We went to the carpark, where there was an old banger of a patrol car, a Citröen, with a cage in the back where the rear seat used to be. They put me into the cage, and the guard had to put my seatbelt on me as I couldn't because of the handcuffs. I wasn't happy with the way they had put them on, as I couldn't raise my hands to my face and replace my mask when it fell down.

We drove cross-country for about forty minutes, with my face mask half off my face. It was an uncomfortable ride, and the car was well overdue for *retirement. Eventually, we arrived at a place called Lodosa, near to Calahorra. I remember being told to bring money with me to get home. Now I understood why: it was a small town in the middle of nowhere. I'd be surprised if they even had a taxi in town, and there'd certainly be no buses home on a Sunday. I was expecting to have to thumb it home tomorrow, knowing full well that nobody would stop for a stranger in times of Covid.*

They took me out of the car and walked me through a building site into a small office. The station was being updated, apparently.

They removed my handcuffs, which had left some deep impressions on my wrists and aggravated my Carpal Tunnel Syndrome. I massaged my wrists.

I was once more spread-eagled and searched, in case I had acquired anything during the journey. There was a cord inside the hood of my hoodie, with a knot at each end. I was told I'd have to remove the cord, or take off my hoodie. I knew the procedure: ironically, I'd saved a girl's life after she'd wrapped such a cord around her neck so tightly in one of my cells when I was a cop. This was the first time I showed any anger during this whole incident. It had been less than a week since I'd attended my brother's funeral, and I can still hear my 80-year-old mother sobbing her broken heart out. Did they really think I would take another of her sons away from her?

I ripped the cord out in anger, gave it to the searching officer, and told him what I thought.

The fat officer in charge took possession of my bag of personal effects. They removed my mask and gave me a new surgical one to wear. They also gave me 'breakfast', which was a small bag of four biscuits, and a small carton of apple juice, minus the plastic straw 'for safety reasons'. I was too stressed to eat, so I put the biscuits in my pocket and drank the juice.

I was told again that they would put me in front of a judge in the morning, or the following morning, if not. I was told CCTV would monitor me throughout my stay.

"Follow me," instructed the fat man.

Now my actual hell began. We crossed the corridor and stepped through a metal door into a smaller, darker, enclosed corridor. I knew instantly where we were, but could hardly believe what I was seeing. There was building material all over the place, and two small doors off to the right. The first one was labelled 'Celda No1' (cell No1). We passed this to the next door, which was Celda No2, opposite of which was a toilet with no door. Clearly visible was a squat hole in the floor for doing your business.

"Press this button if you need anything," he said, before closing the door on me.

I stood still and took in my new surroundings. To say the room was small is an understatement. It was a little longer than it was wide, approximately two by three metres. I could easily touch both walls with my outstretched hands across the width, whereas the length was just out of reach. Along the left wall was a small platform with a mattress on top. This was about bath-sized. Next to that was a small floor space, about a third the width of the bed. I could just about walk four paces to the far wall, and four paces back again. The bed platform had a thin mattress on it, encased in a black, hard plastic cover. There was a similar 'pillow'. On top of this lay a single, scrunched-up, horrific looking blanket. The mattress was too big for the platform, and extended about twenty-five centimetres over the edge, obstructing both the floor space and the door, which opened inwards. I realised that it would be really easy to roll over on to that bit, and fall off the bed onto the hard marble floor, which would hurt as it was quite a drop.

The walls were covered with ceramic tiles in a baby poo colour. There was nothing else in that tiny room. I could probably fit four or five rooms in one of my bathrooms at home. I wouldn't have kept a dog in there.

I turned and looked at the door. It was a thick metal door – ice cold to touch. In fact, the entire room was freezing. There was no evidence of any heating at all. The door had two square viewing/ventilation holes: one at the bottom and one at eye level. A metal mesh had been welded over each one. Above the door was a small, mesh-covered recess with a low level light bulb. The cell was very dark. Next to the bulb was a small CCTV camera, covering the whole cell.

I paced up and down the small cell to take stock of my situation. I don't recall doing what I had been accused of. It was my word against hers. There were no supporting bruises to back up her word. She had tried to cancel the police. Now I was to be kept in this tiny, freezing cell – possibly until Monday? To what end? This was a prison sentence.

For the next few hours I couldn't rest. I paced backwards and forwards, sometimes coming to rest with my forehead against the cold hardness of the opposite wall. It gave me some sort of comfort – a connection with reality, as the whole situation seemed too unreal to comprehend.

At 9.49am, my watch beeped. I glanced at it. It was an update on a WhatsApp group, cancelling the planned visit to a bodega (winery). I was minded to write 'because the driver is in jail' on it, but I resisted. My watch should have been taken off me during the search, and it was clearly still within range of my phone in the office. I could connect with the outside world through my watch!

Having a watch also meant I could keep track of the time, as there was absolutely nothing to help me do this: I couldn't see any daylight at all. I could just about see out of the door grill up to the cell block door, which was a permanently closed metal door. There were male voices on the other side of it, but without the watch, I'd be lost.

By 1.00pm, I was feeling the cold so much that I was shivering. The filthy blanket stared up at me from the bed, but I couldn't bear to touch it, nor the bed. I was still standing up. I was also starving, as I hadn't eaten since dinner the night before (about sixteen hours earlier), although I still had the four biscuits given to me for 'breakfast', but my mouth was so dry I couldn't eat them.

I seriously considered asking for my consulate to be notified of my arrest, as is my right, as I didn't think they should keep a British subject in such conditions, but it was Sunday. Nothing would probably come of it until Monday, anyway.

I remembered my watch and needed to talk to somebody. I looked up my niece and discovered that I could dictate a message to her, which the watch would send as a text message. I whispered into the watch, telling her where I was, how cold I was, and of my hunger.

A few minutes later she replied but, without my glasses, I couldn't even read what she said. A short time later, I got an audio message from my wife, *but I couldn't open that either.*

Within five or ten minutes of sending that message, the guard came to the cell and asked me for my watch. I do not know how he knew I had it, unless they'd seen it on the CCTV, but I'd been quite careful with it so they wouldn't see it.

At this time, though, I was fast approaching the worst experience of my incarceration.

I felt so cold that I knew I had to make a choice. Get under the blanket, or suffer from hypothermia. I sat on the bed and curled up in the corner, as far out of sight of the ever-watching CCTV as I could. The cold of the wall was still pressing into my back and side, yet I still couldn't bring myself to touch the blanket.

I considered hypothermia as an option – a visit and stay in the hospital was a dream compared to this hellhole. I know about hypothermia. As long as I was still shivering, I'd be all right. If I stopped shivering, that would be dangerous, as that is when my consciousness would be impaired. That is when you need urgent medical help, but these guards were not coming to check on me in my cell like we do in the UK. They relied solely on the CCTV, and that would not spot my hypothermia. If I became hypothermic, I assumed I'd die in there.

With my arms wrapped tightly around myself and my body shaking, I did something the army taught me to do: I fell asleep to escape the discomfort. I dosed, on and off, for what seemed about twenty minutes. It was difficult to know how long, as I no longer had any time reference.

A guard woke me up. It was lunchtime. Rice or lentils? Despite my hunger, neither seemed to be a good option.

I asked him about the time. It was 2.00pm. I needed to pee, so he opened the door and I struggled to walk the few steps to the stinking hole opposite my cell.

He could see that I was not in a good way, and asked me if I was all right. I recognise him now. He had been the guy who had come to Viana to get me and bring me here.

I told him I was freezing, and he said he'd get me another blanket. I struggled to pee. The entire time I knew I was under his observation, and it just wouldn't start. Eventually, I finished and turned to the sink. I washed my hands, but there was no towel. The guard indicated some toilet paper nearby. As there was no bin, I dried my hands and stuffed the wet tissue into my pocket. I tottered back to my door.

The guard asked me again what I wanted to eat. I pointed at the squat hole and asked if it was the only toilet. He said it was. I knew I had another twenty-four hours in here, including the morning, and knew I would need to use that toilet in the squatting position, under the guard's watchful gaze, at some point. The thought of it destroyed me.

"Nothing," I replied. He reminded me I had eaten nothing at all so far. I told him that if I ate, it'd probably mean having to use the squat hole, and I just didn't want to. He told the other guard what I'd said as he arrived with a second blanket. It perplexed him. The friendly guard told him it wasn't 'a part of his culture'. I sensed him sympathising with my situation. He asked about the staff toilet, but the other guard said it wasn't possible.

"Biscuits? A juice and biscuits?"

I gratefully accepted the juice and received another small carton, minus the straw. I was told to step back into the toilet to drink it. They offered me the biscuits, which I declined, stating that I still had some in my cell from breakfast. They looked shocked.

"You can't have ANYTHING in your cell with you!" Guard #2 entered the cell and gave it a full search, bringing out the dangerous biscuits. "These are the rules…"

"Your rules, not my rules," I told them. "I'm a civilian, not a soldier like you."

"First your watch, and now biscuits…?"

"Well, can I suggest you do your jobs better, as I was allowed into the cell with them, and I can't guess what your rules are, can I?" I felt like a sergeant again, telling the troops off.

As I finished my drink, the friendly guard chatted to me. He explained they can be put on a charge for such things, and this is when I realised why policing with soldiers doesn't work. They have absolutely no power of discretion; no free will, no decisions to make, and they just follow orders like automatons. Policing is a sensitive job with an infinite amount of variations for every situation, which requires tact, care, common sense, and wise decisions. They aren't permitted to use any of these human qualities.

The friendly guard was almost apologetic as he returned me to my cell. I nodded at the excuse for a toilet, the disorderly corridor, and the tiny, freezing cells. "We have some of these in England too," I said. "We call them museums, though."

I went back into my cell and stood in the corner, wondering how I would cope until morning with no food and such debilitating cold. The friendly guard came back and wheeled a small radiator up to the cell door.

I thanked him, but wasn't sure what difference it would make, as they placed it on the outside of a ten centimetre thick door, and the heat from it needed to penetrate my cell. I returned to pacing the floor and was incapable of comprehending if thirty minutes had passed – or three hours. After a while, though, the cell felt as though the artic edge had been taken off. Eventually, I returned to my corner and tried to doze.

I woke up, completely unsure of what time it was. The radiator had been removed from the door, and I could hear voices in the office. Surely it was about 2.00am or later, as that would mean being closer to getting out of the cell? I began my pacing again, listening for any clue as to what the time was.

My guess was that it was very late in the night. Perhaps the night-shift had come on duty and, finding the office cold, had taken the radiator into the office for their own use.

Without the radiator, the cell was frosty again, and I knew I had no choice – I'd have to get under a blanket to get through the long, freezing night. I thought of how to organise the bed, to make it as comfortable as humanely possible. If I did that, then went to the loo, I could sleep for the rest of the night. Time would pass more quickly. I knew I had to do it; I had no choice.

Eventually, I rang the bell to use the loo.

Silence.

After a few minutes, I rang it again.

Nothing.

I realised that there was now nobody in the office – that I was *completely alone in the cell block, locked in a cell. I felt slightly panicky. What if there was a fire?*

I waited for five minutes and rang it again – this time a bit more aggressively. A guard appeared at the far door and shouted angrily at me, asking me what I wanted. I told him. He shouted again, something fast and incomprehensible, before slamming the door. All I got was the word 'wait'.

I waited for a long time. It felt like thirty minutes, and still nothing. I rang again.

"What?" he shouted.

"Piss! Now!" I shouted back. Two guards finally came and opened the door, and I went to the hole and emptied my bladder. I washed my hands at the sink – the water was ice cold and there was no soap or towel. I used toilet paper to dry my hands again, and put it in my pocket afterwards, wondering if they would be angry with me for taking that into the cell.

I asked them the time as I re-entered the cell, hoping for a really late hour.

"22.45."

So early? My heart sank.

They also pointed out that I hadn't had dinner. In fact, I hadn't been offered anything since 2.00pm, nearly nine hours ago. I was starving, but again, I declined.

I stood and stared at the bed again, thinking of how best to make it up, when all the lights went out in the cell – I was plunged into total darkness!

I was stunned – I couldn't even see my hand in front of my face. One guard told the other that they needed to see me on the CCTV, so the lights came back on, thankfully.

I laid a blanket over the frigid plastic of the mattress and pillow, and climbed on top. The mattress might as well have been made of wood, it was so hard. I pulled the other blanket over me, dreading waking up and discovering that I was still locked up in this dog kennel.

I instantly fell asleep.

Later, I woke up, and listened. What was the time? How long had I been asleep? Five minutes? Five hours? I had no idea. I hoped it was about 10.00am as it would be close to seeing-the-judge-time. I lay in the bed's warmth, again listening for any clue. Nothing.

I felt the need for a pee coming on, and was relieved I didn't feel the 'other' need at all. My stomach rumbled.

Maybe I should ring the bell, in case it takes hours for them to come again like last time? No point in waiting until I'm desperate again.

I rang, and a guard asked me what I wanted. He told me I couldn't come out of the cell, as he was on his own, and they had to have two guards at all times to open the cell door.

I laughed. "So get somebody then – I need a piss!"

"Wait fifteen minutes," he said, then he told me it was eight o'clock in the morning.

Thirty minutes passed and still nothing. I was getting angry. I could hold it, but that wasn't the point. What if I had been desperate…?

I rang again and was told to wait again. He approached my cell door and, speaking through the grill, explained that he was waiting for a patrol to get back in.

I asked him if he had a pistol.

"I do, yes. Why do you ask?"

"Well, draw that pistol, and stand at the end of the corridor whilst I step out of this cell and take a piss in that hole opposite. If you feel threatened at all by me, you have my permission to shoot me."

He looked at me, clearly unsure if I was joking or not.

I wasn't.

Shortly afterwards, two big guards with two big guns let me out for a piss. One explained I would be in front of the judge in the first hour of the morning. My heart leapt… and what time is that, exactly?

"Twelve o'clock."

I laughed at them. "That is actually the last hour of the morning, just before it becomes the afternoon – the clue is in the name. In England, the first hour is about nine."

He told me that, at about eleven o'clock, I would be transferred to a town called Estella, and then taken up to see the judge.

It felt much closer now. Maybe I'd go back to sleep and pass the time faster?

"Want some breakfast?"

I knew what was on offer.

"I'd love some, thanks! Sausage, bacon, and a fried egg with a coffee? Maybe some fresh orange juice?"

He shook his head seriously. "Biscuits."

"No thanks, that's not a breakfast."

A few hours later, I was taken out of my cell, spread-eagled and searched again. They handcuffed me once more, the guard saying he'd do it to my front, and not my back. I hadn't even considered them doing it to my back, and I may well have fought them had they tried to.

They escorted me to a waiting crap-car and caged me in the back again. We drove for about thirty minutes with the guards politely chatting to me through the perspex barrier, asking me questions about the English language, such as how do you say 'yard' in Spanish – as in Scotland Yard. It was difficult to hear over the whine of the engine and the rattles of the cage and car.

In the middle of nowhere, they activated their blue lights and siren and began overtaking traffic on a country road. We were obviously running late. I realized they did not know how to work the buttons for the sirens and lights, and the driver had had no training on how to drive on blues-and-twos. The car was also woeful for the job, wallowing all over the road, with very little engine performance. A few times he overtook and scared the hell out of me. I realised that if we did crash, I'd be trapped in this cage in the back of the car and wouldn't be able to get out. I quickly noted that the car was a diesel and not a petrol car, and hoped that if we did crash, it'd be into another diesel car and there'd be no fire.

Before long, we arrived at Estella, and pulled into the yard of the police station I'd passed several times when going to my niece's college just up the hill. They took me out of the car, and I was shame-walked, in handcuffs, along a queue of citizens lining up outside of the firearms licensing office. They all looked at the handcuffs and then at my eyes, trying to identify what hideous crime I was guilty of. I was glad of the mask concealing my face, and resisted the urge to bite dramatically towards one of the curious onlookers, like some deranged Hannibal Lecter might have done.

We entered a room, and we were swiftly turned around and sent back along the queue for a second time to another room. There they fully fingerprinted and photographed me, like a common criminal, and took me back to the police car.

We drove the short distance up the hill to the courthouse I'd visited before for various reasons, and entered the underground carpark. We were the only people there. They walked me to a cell with bars instead of doors and took off the handcuffs. A short time later, they escorted me upstairs, without handcuffs, where I met my lawyer again. He briefed me on what was about to happen, and what I should say.

We entered the courtroom, and they directed me to a chair in the centre of the room with a small microphone pointed at me. The magistrate read me some crap, and I nodded at all the right places. After about twenty seconds, I was told I was free to go.

Outside the courtroom, they gave me my possessions back, and I immediately called my niece, who was studying a few hundred metres away. I hoped we'd go back home on the bus together, as I seriously needed some loving company right then.

She told me she was at home, looking after the dogs. I cried. It was the first sign I had that my dogs were still at my home, waiting for me, and that they hadn't been some part of a crazy power play where they had been taken away from me.

The café I found at the bus station was open for breakfast. I ordered a coffee and something to eat, then immediately went to the toilet and did what I needed to do, without the fear of being observed throughout the process. When I saw that there wasn't any toilet paper, I almost laughed. I searched my pocket and found the damp pieces of tissue paper I'd dried my hands on earlier.

I devoured my breakfast and savoured the coffee. I then texted my brothers and told them what had happened. Richard replied, "Bloody hell, Dave! What a shit week you're having!"

Burying a brother, and then getting unjustly locked up in a medieval way for almost two days? Yeah. You might describe it like that.

Within the hour, I was finally back home – almost thirty-six hours after being dragged away by the police. Thankfully, my wife had left the house *and was living temporarily in a flat in the nearby city of Logroño. I was not ready to see her just yet.*

My niece had made me a delicious lunch, and – for some weird reason – I just couldn't eat it. I lit a fire to chase out the cold still creeping around in my old bones and got quite drunk.

It was the final nail in the coffin of our marriage. There was no going back after what happened that day. Perhaps it needed something like this to happen for me to move on with my life.

At that point, there were still seventeen days of the awful year of 2020 left, and I intended to stay in my house and just blot out the rest of the year, which I more or less accomplished.

Wednesday 16 December 2020

I signed up to an online war game that my brother Peter had been playing for years, as I knew we could play together. I just hated the thought of him sitting in that house, surrounded by Paul, and yet all alone. It would give us a chance to be together each night, and would distract him from his loneliness. We began playing nightly and, because of the game's complexity, Pete had to coach me on how to play. I hoped it would give him some kind of purpose for a while. We did this regularly for the next few months.

Wednesday 23 December 2020

My home town local paper, *The Uttoxeter Echo*, ran a full-page on my success as a writer. I was really pleased, and I hoped it might give my hurting mum and my brothers a lift, as it had me.

Christmas week came, and Nath took a flight to the Canary Islands to spend the holidays with her boyfriend who lived there, leaving me alone at home with my dogs. I welcomed the time on my own with my thoughts. Besides, my region had gone into lockdown again, and I couldn't leave the province – not that I felt like it, anyway. I spent Christmas week drinking heavily, playing online with Pete, and going for ever-longer runs, just as I had when Paul died.

Thursday 31 December 2020

On the last day of that cursed year, I did a ten-kilometre run, and seriously considered preparing for a future marathon to raise funds for cancer, all in Paul's name. I drank goodbye to the old year, cursed it, and hoped that 2021 might be a better year for all of us.

I could never have predicted what might happen in 2021, but this new year was to usher in the biggest change of my life to date.

CHAPTER 5

2021

Sunday 3 January 2021

The new year started with heavy snowfalls in my area, but I kept on running, regardless. I routinely went for long runs up the hills, and on this day, I actually got lost. I was running across snow-covered, wet vineyards, in strong, icy-cold winds. The meltwater had fully infiltrated my trainers, and I briefly thought I might die up there if I didn't find my way back quickly, and get out of the killer wind. I didn't reach my target of fourteen kilometres, but I survived, although my knees suffered badly. Time to lay off jogging for a bit.

Wednesday 6 January 2021

Quietly drinking from the safety of my sofa, I watched the US imploding as The Capitol was stormed. I listened whilst being warmed by a blazing log fire and the love of my three dogs.

Nath came back and revelled in the snow. Being Brazilian, she'd never seen it before, so we built a large snow-penguin together in the back garden, which took weeks to melt away.

January passed by in a flurry of nothingness.

Friday 29 January 2021

Whilst plodding back from the supermarket, I was about to leave the village and head home when, in an instant, I changed direction, having seen a couple of people I vaguely knew. I engaged them in conversation, despite not feeling like talking to anybody.

That decision was to change the entire course of 2021 for me, and probably the rest of my life.

I'm talking about Wes and Sherry, the Canadians. I'd met them before, as they ran the café on the *Camino de Santiago* in the heart of *Viana*. Their café differed from all the local Spanish cafés, as they seemed to be focused on serving and helping tired pilgrims from all over the world.

I'd stuck my head in their place last year, when I saw a sign outside advertising craft beer. *Seriously? Craft beer? In my village?* I entered and spoke to them, and discovered that they were Canadian and spoke English. In fact, they hardly spoke any Spanish at all. And they didn't have any craft beer for me either. I told them that if they got some craft beers, I'd definitely go back. They did, but I didn't. I hadn't really seen them since, although I'd spotted them recently, riding around on electric bikes.

They were sitting at a table on the pavement, where I left *Viana* to go home. It was their two enormous, fat-tyred mountain bikes, propped against the wall, that had caught my attention. I was curious, so my route to the ramp leading down to my house was interrupted, as I abruptly altered course and made my way towards them. I don't know why I did it, as I wasn't really feeling like talking to anybody. My depression was terrible, and I just wanted to stay away from people.

After some friendly chit-chat about the bikes, they invited me to sit at their table with them. I was very alone and down, and had nothing else to do, so I sat down and chatted.

It was just seven weeks since Paul's funeral, and my subsequent inhuman incarceration, and the long-overdue conclusion of my second marriage. Christmas had come and gone unnoticed, and I was drinking a lot. My wife never returned to the home, so we were officially separated, yet her niece stayed with me. She said that she didn't want to live in a flat in *Logroño*, but I think she also wanted to monitor me. I'm so glad that she did.

Wes and Sherry were very engaging, and quick to listen, so it wasn't long before I told them I was reeling from the sudden loss of my brother, and that my marriage had ended too. It felt good to tell people – even complete strangers. They offered me a drink, but I didn't want to outstay my welcome, nor did I feel like it: it would mean trying to be sociable, and I just wasn't capable of doing that.

So I thanked them and went home.

> *Extract from the journal of Wes, 29 January 2021:*
> *"While we were sitting there, Dave, the guy who had the English academy, came and sat down with us. He said he had had a very hard November, as he lost a brother to lung cancer, and another brother has cancer, and is going through chemotherapy. Father, thank You for the opportunity we had to listen to Dave. I pray he will find You in the midst of this grief. Lord, I pray for more opportunities to be able to share with Dave. After Dave left, R**** stopped and had a coffee with us. Thank You, Lord, for the fact that these people crossed our path. I truly believe, Lord, You directed this."*

My ex and I agreed a way forward: she would get our academy business in its entirety, whilst I got to stay at the marital home with the three dogs. The arrest had triggered an automatic divorce procedure, which we both agreed to.

During February and March, I had to distract myself from my pain. I was struggling to deal with the loss of Paul, as was my family. My marriage breakdown was an additional burden to bear: I'd lost a wonderful friend – perhaps my only genuine friend – and was thrown into financing my large home and niece, with just a single source of income now. Although that was just one more worry, it was refreshing to be away from the unpredictability of the life I'd been living for the last twenty years.

I wasn't writing at all – it had all dried up. My increasing depression was preventing me from putting any words down on paper. Instead, I bought a lot of products online, and tried to bury myself in improving my home. I had also continued to go for runs, in memory of Paul.

> *Extract from the journal of Wes, 5 February 2021:*
> *"While going to buy some groceries, we ran into David, the guy from the UK, and visited with him also. Thank You, God, for bringing these people in our path today."*

My life basically consisted of heavy drinking, longer runs, and occasional meetups with the ex. Meanwhile, my brother Mick was fighting his own battle against cancer, losing two stones in weight and struggling to cope with the treatment – aggressive chemo and radiotherapy. He was in and out of hospital and nearly threw the towel in at one point. He had to be encouraged to continue with his treatment by his wife.

Spring arrived and my large garden burst into flower. This year would be different though, as I couldn't bring myself to do any work in it. I'd failed to plant any vegetables whatsoever. It just didn't seem important to me.

Saturday 6 March 2021

In the evening, Nath and I went to the café run by Wes and Sherry – *The Pilgrims' Oasis* in *Viana*. It was good to talk to them, although I was worried about their religious background. I didn't want to be preached at, or for somebody to try to convert me, especially as I was down and perhaps perceived to be vulnerable. I made it clear from the outset that I wasn't there for any kind of talk of religion, but Sherry quickly responded that they weren't religious.

I was perplexed.

"No," she said. "We're just followers of Jesus."

Ergo, religious! "So, what are you, then? Mormons or something?" I asked, totally lost.

She laughed. "No, we're not. Look, Dave, it's not about religion, it's about having a relationship with Jesus."

I thought *she* was confused. "Look, I'm sorry, but I hate religion."

"So do we!" She smiled back at me. "*And so did Jesus!*"

Now this was getting silly. How can *Jesus* hate religion, and how can *she* hate religion when *her* religion *was* Jesus?

I needed a drink.

In the end she seemed to understand my point of view more than I did hers, and it felt safe enough for me to invite them back to our house for pizza that night, as a kind of thank you for helping me through the difficult times.

> *Extract from the journal of Wes, 6 March 2021:*
> *"In the evening shift, Dave and his niece came in until closing. He asked us over to his place for pizza, so we went and stayed until curfew at 11. Dave is hurting from the loss of his brother and also from his divorce that just went through. Lord, give us opportunities to share Your love with him."*

Wednesday 10 March 2021

My neighbour crashed her car into my new garden fence. I had to pursue her for the compensation, and repair the fence, something that was just so unnecessary for me, and something I wished I didn't have to do.

Later that week, I went to the café and gave Wes and Sherry (who I will, from here on, refer to as 'the Canadians') a copy of my published book, *The Rozzers*, about my life as a police officer in the UK. They were very thankful to me.

Meanwhile, the lawyer of my ex sent me emails, saying I was denying her access to the house, which was ridiculous.

The two e-bikes that the Canadians owned, which had brought me across to their table back in January, impressed me so much that I contemplated buying one too. Then my ex ordered one and asked me to assemble it for her. I did, and took it for a test drive with the Canadians, riding along tracks to a distant village and back. I loved it so much that I ordered one for myself online.

The end of March was up and down for me. I attended my ex's

birthday party, as a friend, and began doing some long-overdue DIY jobs around the home to keep busy.

March turned into April, and I was spending more and more time visiting *The Oasis café* and chatting with the Canadians. As the season for the pilgrims was warming up, more and more pilgrims came into the café, and I began to engage with some of them too.

The Canadians and I went on bike trips together, visiting villages around my home town that I didn't even know existed, despite having lived there for ten years. My ex and I had spent those ten years working long and hard days, just to ensure that our company prospered.

Eventually, after one such outing, the Canadians invited me back to their house. They had pizza, and, after all that cycling, I was starving. The three of us sat at the table in front of mounds of steaming pizza – there is nothing like the smell of pizza when you are starving – and I was just about to tuck in, when Wes said, "I'd like to pray."

Before I could react, he bowed his head and started talking to God!

This was just the thing I was very fearful of, and, whilst I have no problem at all with people having whatever belief they have, I really didn't want it to be forced on me.

My reaction, unfortunately, was a very rude one.

> Sherry: "As Wes started praying, Dave obviously wasn't expecting it, and reacted to it badly, blurting out, 'I'll have no part of that!' Wes, however, just continued on with the prayer and Dave didn't know what to do. When Wes had finished, I told him that Dave obviously didn't want him to pray, but Wes said he had started so he'd finish it. I think Wes' words had had an impact on Dave, though, as he had thanked God for Dave and his friendship. The next time Dave came around, we didn't pray, as we knew how he felt about it, but on the third visit, he came with Nath, and we asked them if we could pray this time. They both said yes."

I think this interaction is a clear indication of two things: how low and how lost I was, and just where I stood in relation to all things religious.

Wednesday 14 April 2021

My neighbour crashed into my garden fence *again*, which I'd only just replaced from the previous damage she'd caused, but this time she denied all knowledge – despite having been filmed on my security cameras doing it!

My niece slowly and surely became my saviour, looking after me and lifting me with her humour and infectious drive and energy. Despite being only 21 years old, Nath grew wise quickly and was extremely supportive of me. She grew up so much in that awful year.

My new bike arrived at the end of April, and I instantly fell in love with it.

As the six-month anniversary of the death of my brother approached, I felt his loss more and more. I was having so much difficulty coming to terms with it. Even so, or maybe because of this, the Canadians took me out on bike rides several times a week, and I began exploring on my own too. The bike gave me a sense of freedom and exhilaration that I was so desperately in need of, plus a plentiful amount of solitude, as I still wasn't very sociable towards people.

Tuesday 18 May 2021

WhatsApp message to Nathalia:
Me: "These lyrics from one of my favourite songs (by Meatloaf¹) always remind me of you: 'Oh, baby you're the only thing in this whole world that's pure and good and right, and wherever you are and wherever you go, there's always gonna be some light…"

I cannot describe how much she helped me through this period. She was the light that kept me going through the darkest of days.

However, my depression was about to go into overdrive, and take me to a place I never thought I'd see.

Saturday 22 May 2021

I had to do a Spanish language exam in a nearby city, in order to apply for a Spanish passport. Over lunch, I sent Nath a message telling her how

I'd got on, and she replied that she was proud of me. I downplayed my results, as they should have been much better for the time I'd been living in Spain. She replied, "I'm *always* proud of you…"

I sat in a square in the town of *Tudela,* with tears streaming down my face.

The next day, my ex and I took Nath to *San Sebastian* on the coast for an early birthday present. My ex apologised to us both for her actions, and we got on really well as a family, and had some great food and *Cava.* She was getting the help she needed, whilst I was slowly sinking beneath the surface.

Through the end of May and into June, I used the bike a lot, and began going on several longer rides with my ex, as she was getting really worried about my state of mind.

Tuesday 22 June 2021

The three of us – my ex, Nath, and I – went into *Logroño* to watch a game of football together: England were playing against the Czech Republic in the European Championships (Euros 2020), which had been postponed from the previous year because of the pandemic. England had been doing very well so far, so my hopes were cautiously rising for some sporting success for my national team.

Unfortunately, for various reasons, that night was a disaster, and I ended up missing most of the game (England beat Czech Republic 1-0).

I was really annoyed with my ex the following day, as everybody we knew was talking about the unexpected win, which I didn't get to see. It meant that England were now up against Germany in the last sixteen, and my spirits lifted slightly, although the prospect of playing against Germany was, as always, very daunting.

I was, however, determined not to miss the next game.

Wednesday 23 June 2021

I went to the café as usual to have a coffee and hang out a bit. The place is right in the centre of the village, right on the *Camino de Santiago.* Whilst sitting at the tables outside, you get to see every pilgrim passing through the village, with the option of engaging them in conversation.

The Pilgrims' Oasis café, Viana, Navarra

The Canadians told me that a friend of theirs was visiting that day: Ben from Holland. I suspected Ben was also religious, as they really wanted me to meet him. The Canadians confirmed he had found Jesus and had a very interesting story to tell. *Interesting for you*, I thought.

As the day was so beautiful, I sat outside enjoying the warm sun on my face, and watched the people as they were passing by.

Eventually Ben arrived, and he sat at my table. I politely greeted him, but watched him warily. Before long, my suspicions were confirmed. A passing pilgrim sat down and had a drink with us. Within minutes, Ben was telling her 'his story'. I did not know that 'your story' meant the story of how a person had found God.

As soon as I heard him talking about Jesus, I buried my head in a book that was on the table, and pretended to be reading it, not listening to his story. Seriously, I didn't want any God-talk, and assumed that once the lady heard the name 'Jesus' she'd be up and gone too, and then Ben would politely change the subject.

However, she loved 'his story', so Ben continued on enthusiastically.

I needed to escape without seeming rude. His story obviously mattered to him, but I cared little for any talk of religion.

"Oh, I have a hair appointment!" I announced, placing the book down. "Sorry, gotta go!" I got up and walked the one hundred metres to the local barbershop, hoping that Ben wasn't aware that they didn't take appointments.

"I'm busy. Come back in twenty minutes," replied the barber.

As I walked back to the café, I could see Ben and the girl in deep, huddled conversation. As I reached their table, I heard the name 'Jesus' again, and immediately turned left and entered the café.

Sherry greeted me. "Are you okay?"

"Yeah, thanks, but I really need to get a haircut. I've got to go back in twenty minutes."

"Do you want a drink while you wait? You can have it outside, with Ben."

"No!" I hissed, rather too urgently, whilst glancing back at the open door to make sure Ben hadn't heard me.

"Oh, really? Why not?" Sherry was concerned.

"He's preaching! About Jesus! I don't want *anybody* talking to me about any religion!"

Sherry laughed. "Dave, it's not *about* religion…"

"I know, I know," I interjected sarcastically.

"It's about a *relationship*."

"– *relationship*."

We said the last word simultaneously, only I said it with derision.

Sherry laughed at my reaction.

Sherry: "And still do!"

I breathed out and relaxed a little at her good-natured response. "Look, Sherry, just so you know, you will *never* convert me."

"*We* don't do the converting, *Jesus* does. And *never* say never!"

Wes was listening to the conversation from behind the counter, and came to Ben's defence.

"You know, Ben has a very interesting story, and he is very passionate about it."

I don't recall saying this at all, but my tone apparently changed as I replied, "I actually envy that kind of passion…"

> Ben: "*Dave was sitting outside the bar when I arrived. Wes had told me he might be. He wasn't a Christian, but respected others' views, but absolutely wanted no preaching at him. I sat and had a drink with him. I felt great compassion for him, as he'd had a hard time. I was very careful not to speak of my faith with him, but then an opportunity too good to miss arose: a pilgrim sat with us! I told her I'd travelled around the world in search of an answer to life when I was younger. She asked me if I had an answer, so I had to tread carefully, as Dave was still at the table. I tried to be careful to talk of my personal relationship with Jesus, and not of an impersonal religion. As expected, Dave soon fled the table and walked off up the street. Wes later said that Dave had told them he hated being preached to by me, but had admired my passion. I was glad of his reaction, as it beats an indifferent response. Dave was clearly not indifferent, which motivated me to pray for him even more.*"

Tuesday 29 June 2021

I watched the England and German game alone, in a bar in my village. It was just me and a disinterested barman. England beat Germany 2-0. The fact that I was sitting all alone during such an important game was clearly indicative of my life at that time. That I was desperate for some good football news to lift me showed how miserable my life had become.

Wednesday 30 June 2021

The following day, I spoke to the Canadians at the café, and they excitedly reminded me that their new volunteer was due to arrive in the village on Thursday. Perhaps I'd like to come up and meet her on Friday, once she had settled in, and been brought up to the café?

I knew she was a Christian, and probably a missionary – it seemed that all of their friends were believers. I remember asking myself why they didn't have any 'normal' friends, and I seriously didn't want to meet any *missionary*. But, a promise is a promise, so I went.

I didn't know how much my mood – in fact, my whole life – was about to be changed.

PAGE 53
[1] "Bat out of Hell" by Meatloaf.
Singer: Martin Lee Aday.
Songwriter: Jim Steinman.
Producer: Todd Rundgren.
Lyrics: © Carmen America Inc, Warner Chappell Music Inc.

CHAPTER 6

A NEW FRIEND

Thursday 1 July 2021

Wes and Sherry drove to *Bilbao*, in the north of Spain, to collect the new volunteer from the airport and bring her back to *Viana*.

> *Kate: "When I arrived in Spain, Wes and Sherry met me at Bilbao airport. As we drove the ninety minutes to Viana, we chatted about what lay ahead at the café. They spoke about Dave, saying that he was 'a friend, but he didn't want to hear about any of that Jesus stuff'. I prayed for him there and then, in the back of the car. I prayed he would come to know the truth, that God would soften his heart to receive the truth, and that the Holy Spirit would work in him and bring him into the light."*

Friday 2 July 2021 – The Oasis café, Viana, Navarra, Spain

It was evening time, and I'd made a commitment to go. Reluctantly, Nath and I walked up to The Oasis café to see the Canadians and have a coffee with them, and to meet the new member of staff: Kate, the volunteer.

I didn't know what a missionary did, although I had a stereotypical view of one, which was very unflattering. I didn't really feel like meeting her at all.

The Canadians were very sociable, but I wasn't. I had never really been all that friendly, and with this awful depression, I was less inclined to meet anybody at all. Socialising was the last thing I wanted to do, but I couldn't let them down, regardless of how I was feeling.

We entered the café alone and were confronted with two young, unknown women sitting opposite each other, near the door. Wes and Sherry were sitting just beyond them. Sherry seemed to lead the conversation with the two ladies. Presumably, one of the two was the new volunteer, although it surprised me it wasn't readily obvious. As for the other lady, I didn't know who she might be.

I really didn't want to have to speak to people, especially strangers. The Canadians would have been acceptable, but now there were *two* new people for me to have to deal with.

Oh, why did I come..?

I smiled politely and said hi to everybody, and waited to be introduced to the new girl, but no introduction was forthcoming from Wes or Sherry. So I tried to work out which of the two women she might be, and who the other one was. I knew Kate was an American, so her accent would clearly give her away. Perhaps the other girl was a pilgrim, as most customers there were, especially if they were speaking English?

The girl on the left looked late teens and was very animated, and very talkative. She was speaking in near-perfect English, and had a light American accent. The girl to the right appeared slightly older, and spoke perfect English, but she also spoke with a very light American accent. She was the quieter of the two.

I dusted my detective skills off and put them to good use: lady to the left? *Late teens?* Too young to be walking the *camino* alone. *Talkative?* Definitely American. *Accent?* American. *Animated?* American.

That must be Kate then, and the quieter girl on the right, perhaps a pilgrim.

I got it completely wrong. The chatty girl was a local girl called Ana[2], who was preparing for a Cambridge English exam (the B2 First Certificate) the following day. Her accent came from her time spent studying in the US. Kate was the quiet one sitting on the right.

It just happened that the exam Ana was preparing for was the same exam I had been teaching for the past twenty years. There wasn't anything I didn't know about that exam, despite quitting teaching a year earlier. It was also apparent that Sherry was trying to guide her on how to pass the exam, and it was also clear Sherry didn't really know anything about that exam.

So, feeling useful, I stepped up and helped her out.

I had been very passionate about teaching students how to pass that exam, and with some incredible success over the years. Many of my students passed the exam who shouldn't really have passed it at all! I knew all the tricks and techniques required to gain an advantage, and this was why I excelled with my students. Some students who had the B2 level often gained the higher C1 certificate through my guidance.

I knew instantly that Ana had a very high level of English, and would clearly pass the exam (notwithstanding her abilities in writing and grammar), but I also knew that it would be possible for her to get a higher level than the B2 if she got great results.

The old, passionate teacher in me came to the fore, and I gave her as much help as I could, hoping that she might take it all in, and achieve the higher level pass. She had spent a lot of time in the States, and was well accustomed to American English, but she wasn't as comfortable with my 'type' of English – *British* English. When I told her the examiners would probably be British (I knew most of them), she seemed to be genuinely panicky. I tried to soothe her fears by explaining that both versions of English were acceptable in the Cambridge exams.

Kate, meanwhile, just watched my teacher-show. At some point, she said that she was just enjoying my British accent, and I commented on how most Americans loved our accent. I referenced a scene from the TV series *Friends*, where Ross puts on a British accent when filling in temporarily as a lecturer at university. Kate said the fact that I had just referenced *Friends* meant that she and I were going to be great friends, which was very prophetic of her.

I thought I was doing really well regarding both ladies. However, when I later asked Kate to recall her first impression of me for this book, she had a slightly different view of the interaction.

Kate: "You seemed to be a cranky British man who couldn't even be bothered with a proper greeting for the new girl. Extremely pompous, and clearly enjoying feeling superior, as you barked instructions to a shaking, intimidated 16-year-old girl. I felt you were desperate for significance, and fiercely unhappy."

During the conversation, the ongoing football competition briefly came up. I spoke of how many times we might see a foul being committed in the game, but Ana didn't know the word *foul*, and mistakenly heard me say *owl* instead. She asked me what I had meant by *an owl being committed*. We all laughed at her error, and then I corrected her misunderstanding, and explained what a *foul* meant in a game of football.

Sherry joked with her about hearing the word *owl*, and tried to explain to Ana what an owl was, comically using the sound an owl makes. As she did so, for reasons unknown to me, I turned and glanced at the open doorway to the café. It took me a while to comprehend what I was seeing.

Just outside, on the pavement, in direct line of sight of me, was a man in the street. Nothing unusual in that, except for the enormous, live, Eagle Owl perched regally on his right hand.

"There!" I cried, jumping to my feet, incredulous. "*That's* an owl!"[3] None of us could believe the coincidence of seeing a real, live owl in the café doorway, just as we were trying to explain what one was. What are the chances of that happening? The odds of this coincidence are astronomical.

This was probably the most amazing coincidence I had ever witnessed, but such things were about to become a big part of my life – routine almost – and I wouldn't be able to figure out what was going on for quite some time.

After a short while, I made my excuses and bid them all goodnight, and returned to the safety of my home.

That evening, as I was discussing the owl story with Nath, she noticed I seemed much happier than I had been in a while, and she was curious why.

I instantly realised that I did indeed feel happier, but I didn't know why I did. She suggested it might have been because of the teaching of the exam to Ana, and that perhaps I missed the 'joy' of teaching? Ever caring, she proposed I should consider starting a course (in English) of self-defence classes for local ladies, to motivate me, to help me feel happier.

I replied with a maybe, but I knew deep down that I really had had quite enough of teaching. It was just too incomprehensible that teaching had somehow lifted my spirit – I was seriously sick of teaching after twenty years, and was so happy to have finally got out of it and 'retired'.

My depression had been so heavy – extremely heavy – for several months, yet something in that visit to the café had definitely just lifted my spirit, for the first time in ages.

I certainly didn't think my sudden joy was anything to do with Kate's arrival, as we had hardly spoken at all, and she seemed like just another person in the café. That night, I didn't consider Kate as the potential source at all.

Saturday 3 July 2021

The following day, England were playing against Ukraine in the quarter-finals of the competition. If they won, they'd go through to the semi-finals. I mentioned it in the café, and Kate asked if she could watch it with me, as she enjoyed 'soccer'. It surprised me that an American lady would enjoy football.

I took Nath with me, and Kate joined us at a nearby bar. Over the game, Kate and I began chatting and getting to know each other.

England won by a large margin, and my spirits rose yet again. Nath and Kate became instantly close, and went out into *Logroño* together one evening.

Over the next few days, I went to the café and spent more and more time chatting with Kate.

Wednesday 7 July 2021

England were playing in a difficult semi-final game against Denmark, and a win would put them through to their first final in living memory. It was an important game, and Kate agreed to meet me again to watch it, although she was visiting the *albergue* at *Villamayor* that day, and would arrive late.

England beat Denmark 2-1 and went through to the final – the first final in decades! I was elated.

After the game, I felt comfortable enough to ask Kate for her phone number and, later that night, we started chatting on *WhatsApp* for the first time:

> *Me to Kate: "… you are pure goodness, and the world needs more people like you."*
>
> *Kate: "… that's so sweet… you've quickly become one of my favourite people in Spain."*

Thursday 8 July 2021

I went to the café to meet up with Kate, and we spent most of the day together, getting to know each other, both in person and on *WhatsApp*. We'd become really close in a very short period.

She was living with the Canadians whilst volunteering at their café and, that evening, they invited me back to their house for dinner.

By this time, Kate had heard all about my writing and books, and that my depression had prevented me from writing a single word in months. She made it her personal mission to get me back to writing, so we arranged a 'writing date' together for the following day at the café. She was a journalist for her organisation, and she needed to be writing too.

That night, I tested out my iPad, and added the new keyboard to it I'd bought the previous year, but had never used. Everything was set, and I spent the evening trying to get in the mood for writing tomorrow.

Friday 9 July 2021

I met up with Kate at the café and took a table in the sun. Kate got little writing done, as friends of the Canadians were visiting, so she was required to be inside with them, rather than outside with me. So I sat outside, thinking of what to write, whilst drinking a glass of wine. I was not ready to go back to my current book, as I would need to re-read everything to pick up where I had left off, so I wrote from the heart about myself and my feelings. Kate came out and checked on me when she could, and sat with me occasionally.

Kate and I, sitting outside The Pilgrims' Oasis, Viana, Navarra

Original text
Written that Friday at the café, as words returned to me once more:

"… and then I saw an angel. A living, breathing, flesh and blood angel, radiating love and goodness and positive energy, a power so strong I instantly felt life returning to my tired old batteries. Within a few days, I felt the sun on my face again. I began to see the beauty of life around me once more. Even words came back to me.

How can one person have such a power? Her hug is like a magical cloak, her smile the radiant sun on my face. Her pushing and prodding completing the course of medicine so perfectly timed. And all this, in just a few days?

An angel, hiding in full view."

This was exactly a week to the day that I had met Kate. My mood had lifted on that previous Friday, and there I was – seven months after quitting writing – sitting in the village and writing again. It was nothing short of miraculous. So I clearly came to the only conclusion that I could come to: Kate was an *angel*. Naively, I later called her an angel to her face, and she quickly shot me down, telling me she'd explain why one day. I had no idea what she was talking about. To me, an angel was a creature of pure goodness, just like her.

Kate's journal: "Dave has been telling me he is a writer but hasn't written anything in seven months. I know people tend to stop doing the things they love when they're depressed, but it feels extra depressing to not be doing the things we love. I convinced him to show up at the café for a writing session together. I also need some encouragement to write, as things have been so crazy the past two weeks that I haven't made it a priority. I've been praying that deep down inside of him, there's some joy left and that writing might awaken that. When he showed up at the café, there was a glimmer of excitement in him, like he had just remembered a part of himself. We sat outside and quietly typed away, and within half an hour or so, he was actually smiling. It was really great to see. I'm praying that he's turned a corner in his depression, and that one day, he'll know genuine joy."

Kate spent the afternoon shopping with Nath in the nearby city of *Logroño*. They later came back to our home where Kate met the dogs, and we spent the evening playing ball with them in the garden. Kate constantly spoke to me of Jesus, and of how He was trying to get my attention, and of how He was working through her to get to me. I totally refused to accept her explanations, and constantly changed the subject at every opportunity, stating that I just did not want to hear about Jesus.

My German Shepherd, Adah, is a very defensive dog, and she barks at everybody who enters our property, regardless of how many months they might have been visiting us. When Kate walked through the gate for the first time, Adah didn't bark at her once – she accepted Kate as if she had known her all her life. To date, Kate is the only person to have done this with Adah.

Nath and I invited Kate and the Canadians to our house for a barbecue on Saturday evening, and agreed to meet up for the football final on Sunday.

Saturday 10 July 2021

The four of us had a delicious barbecue at our home, and Kate stayed later as we chatted in the garden. Again, she spoke of Jesus at every opportunity, and I dismissed it as hocus-pocus.

Sunday 11 July 2021

This was the first day of this whole weird journey that I began to question what was happening to me, and around me. My life was in flux somehow, and I didn't know exactly how or why, just that *something* was happening, and I couldn't put my finger on what or who was responsible for these changes. The little alterations also seemed to be slowly speeding up, and had all started on the day that I'd met Kate.

Kate is an attractive woman and, although she is much younger than me, we had instantly connected, and became good friends when we first met – just nine days earlier. As she later quipped, "I arrived on July 1st, we met on July 2nd, and we were best friends forever on July 3rd."

Obviously, for a person like Kate to become a wonderful friend to me is enough to make a lonely guy thrilled, but, deep down, I suspected the process was something more than just Kate.

Kate had a very clear aura about her – a kind of energy that was hard to miss. Her face glowed in a way I couldn't explain. I'd once worked with a lady who had the same glow. She was a chubby vicar who everybody instantly fell in love with. I once described it as being as if she knew the secrets of the universe.

Kate had that same look, only much stronger. She also had a superpower: she loved to hug people, and, when she did so, you could feel the energy within her, a kind of healing. I watched her many times as she hugged others – complete strangers, the elderly, kids, and dogs. Everybody seemed to feel it. Even my overly protective dog knew! Kate was also extremely wise, far too wise for her years.

There was definitely something 'special' about her. Then there was my instant mood lift. Okay, the football was cheering me up no end, but my mood had lifted inexplicably the night I met her, and I was definitely becoming happier by the day.

And that owl that weirdly appeared when I first met her? Owls are considered messengers or omens in many cultures and religions, and are certainly known to be wise. Was that owl some kind of message that I simply didn't understand?

Me to Kate, 3.00pm: "It's like you are looking right into my soul..."

We all met up for the football final, but England lost the game, and, predictably, I got quite drunk that night, and ended up causing the first argument between the two of us.

As I walked her home after the game, our conversation once more turned to what had been going on in my life since Kate arrived. Kate immediately started talking about Jesus. I told her it wasn't about Jesus – it was about her. I drunkenly told her I could only see her standing in front of me, and not Jesus, and that she was beautiful. I could only believe in what I could see, and I could only see *her* standing there, and *nobody* else!

I told her that what she believed in was a matter for her, and not for me. I could see her, so I could believe in her, and only her. She argued that if I believed in her, then I believed in Jesus.

I thought it ridiculous, and became very frustrated that she batted everything I said away from her, and onto something I didn't – I wouldn't – believe in.

She explained it was like me knowing that a cupcake was real, but not 'believing' in the sugar that was within the cupcake: if the cupcake was real, the sugar had to be real! (Kate was the cupcake, Jesus was the sugar.)

I was quickly learning that arguing with Kate was impossible, as she always had an answer for everything, which invariably made sense. It was frustrating me so much that I felt there was no point in even trying.

As we turned the corner to the street where she lived, I behaved in typical male fashion: I bid her good night and just stood there, watching to see that she reached her door safely. In my strop, I wouldn't walk her *all* the way home.

As soon as I got back to my house, we began chatting on *WhatsApp*, and, after a few messages, we had become best friends again. We chatted extremely late into the night, even though Kate always goes to bed very early and rises early. That was the person she was.

> Me to Kate (Monday 12 July, 3.00am):
> "I see you and I see things I can't explain…"

Monday 12 July 2021

It was no early start for me, on account of my hangover and late night, and I immediately apologised to Kate for keeping her awake until the early hours. Over our conversation, we decided to go on a local hike and have a picnic. Nath was busy, as were the Canadians, so we went ahead on our own, and planned it for the following day.

Tuesday 13 July 2021

We met at my house quite early, and walked out on the *camino* towards *Logroño*, stopping often to take photos. We had a picnic by a lake, then headed back home, hanging out a while at my place. Most of the conversation was about faith, and I let Kate speak without getting annoyed with her this time. I listened more and challenged less. I guess I felt I had been unfair to her on Sunday night, and I tried to show her a better side of me.

That Tuesday evening, Kate suggested the Canadians invite me to something called 'Community Lunch' on Wednesday. I'd heard them mention this before, and speak of some people who had just bought an old monastery to convert to some kind of accommodation.

It sounded interesting, so I accepted the invitation. It felt good to have new friends in my life, and to be visiting unknown places, and making even more new friends. My life had certainly changed in the last two weeks!

In that short period, I had gone from the deepest, darkest depression I have ever known to a much happier place. Yes, I had a new friend in my life, and I felt an energy emanating from her that I just couldn't explain. And yes, my social life was picking up, even if all of my new friends were 'believers'.

My life was indeed changing, and I was really looking forward to visiting the monastery tomorrow, and taking lots of pictures, and eating what was reputed to be fantastic food.

There was no way I could have even conceived of what lay in store for me that day, or the impact it would have on me and my future life.

PAGE 60

[2] Not her real name.

PAGE 62

[3] To see the actual video we took that day of the owl outside the café, follow this link to *Youtube*: https://bit.ly/3OywoH8

CHAPTER 7

WHAT JUST HAPPENED?

Wednesday 14 July 2021

"That's the place!" said Sherry, pointing excitedly, as we pulled up outside a large building in the tiny village of *Barbarin, Navarra*. There were several cars crammed around the entrance to the imposing structure.

"I need to speak to you, Kate," I whispered, as we got out of the car and walked towards the main door. "I feel really weird. I'm not sure what happened to me back there in that church, but I know I need a hug right now."

I seriously needed *something*. Our visit to the disused monastery in *Irache* was over, and I wasn't actually dead, and yet I knew that something really weird had happened to me. I'd felt a sensation that I could only later describe as a pure 'emotion', unlike anything I'd felt before. It was just so distinctly unique to anything I have ever experienced in my 55 years of life, and I couldn't put it into words at the time – I still struggle now.

As we walked towards the second monastery visit of the day, I concluded that the unfamiliar sensation in my chest wasn't actually a *physical* feeling at all – and therefore not a threat to my wellbeing – it was something completely different.

We entered the *Monastery of Barbarin*, which had recently been bought by a Christian organisation called *Oasis Trails*, and was introduced to Jan, a lovely Dutch guy who was the local manager for Oasis Trails. As he gave our group (which included several pilgrims from their *albergue*) a tour of the whole vast complex, I quietly followed on behind. I seriously hoped nothing weird was going to happen inside of this monastery as well.

The place was a photographer's dream! Four storeys high, it was full of incredible paraphernalia, and artefacts, all belonging to the previous inhabitants: old furniture, photos, ID cards, personal letters, rosters, etc. It was like time had just stopped and the occupants had vanished – it was the ideal place to explore and record on film. Yet, I took just *one* photo whilst there! This was of the stunning view across the back garden from an upstairs dormitory.

I'm a hobby photographer. I *always* take loads of photos. At the previous monastery that day, I'd taken sixteen photographs and one video of a place I had *already* visited and photographed *twice* before. Then, shortly afterwards, I visited this monastery *full* of artefacts for the *first* time, and took just *one* photo! But when I returned there a week later for my second visit, I explored the place fully, taking *thirty-nine* photos, including one of a signed letter from Mother Teresa of Calcutta!

My single photo taken on my first visit to the Oasis Trails Monastery

Clearly, something was going on with me. Something was affecting me significantly during that first visit.

After the initial tour, they took us the five-minute ride to Jan's home, where we met his family and other people who worked with him, all busily preparing a lunch in their rear garden. Having only ever met four people with shiny faces in my *whole* life, I suddenly discovered another six over that lunch! There were approximately fifteen people from six different nationalities eating that day. And again, I failed to take a single photo of that event.

Prior to eating, the entire group stood in a large circle and took it in turns to introduce themselves, and say what they were thankful for. Annemieke, Jan's wife, asked who wanted to go first. As I was standing next to her and was their guest, I volunteered.

I gave thanks for Wes and Sherry for their friendship over the previous months, when I had been at rock bottom. They had helped to keep my head above water when I thought I would go under. Then I thanked Kate for yanking me out of the water.

That certainly broke the ice.

Once everybody had finished, we sat down to eat, and broke off into small groups of conversation. I wasn't the only new person there – a couple of pilgrims who were staying at the *albergue* the organisation ran had been invited too.

The food was all home-cooked from locally sourced produce, and it was – just as promised – amazing.

Community Lunch happened every Wednesday, with all the staff and family, many volunteers, pilgrims at the *albergue,* and invited guests. It was to become the highlight of my week for the next few months.

My mood improved considerably over the meal, as the people were just so friendly, and positive, and energising. The weird feeling inside of me seemed to settle down somewhat.

At 4.00pm, we all said our goodbyes, and we four headed off to the nearby village of *Villamayor*, and drove up a steep and windy track behind the village to reach a castle at the top of the hill overlooking the entire area. It was to be my fourth visit, but Kate's first.

On the wall overlooking the entire village and the vast valley is a large bell. Kate spun the bell, and it rang out its melody across the people below – a rejoicing and joyous sound.

When it stopped, I noticed it had some writing on it. I peered in and saw that the bell had been forged in September 1965, some fifty-five years earlier. The exact month that I had been born, coincidentally – maybe even the very day! I'd never noticed that before.

I felt so happy up there, and I took a raft of pictures of Kate and me, of Wes and Sherry, and of the spectacular views. We then headed back down to the village to visit the *albergue* at the foot of the hill, which was run by the same people from lunch.

We met some of the staff we'd eaten with earlier, and had coffee with them and some pilgrims. They asked us if it had been us that had rung the bell above them, as it was clearly audible for many kilometres.

We then visited a lavender field we'd spotted from the castle, where Kate and I laughed and joked and took a multitude of pictures. Soon, it was time to head home. I sat in the back of the car as we drove the thirty minutes along the motorway, staring out of the window. It'd been such a busy day – we had done so much together, but that feeling from the church, six hours earlier, was still in me, and I couldn't figure out what it was. I still needed to discuss this with somebody, and who better than Kate?

When I was dropped off at home, I sent her this message.

Me to Kate, 6.46pm: "Very moving, very special day for me."

Unfortunately, Kate had to travel to Bilbao that night, as she was catching a flight in the morning to Kosovo, and would be away for a week. So, as Kate was on the bus heading to the airport and incommunicado, I later met the Canadians in the village for a drink and discussed some of the day's weird events.

One thing I questioned them about was something I'd witnessed at the meal. A French volunteer at the *albergue* had mentioned that he had a terrible toothache. Two of those present (including Kate) laid hands on him whilst Jan prayed aloud to Jesus to heal him. Then they all carried on as if nothing had happened.

"So, was that a *serious* thing, then?" I asked.

"Of course! Why do you ask?" replied Sherry, laughing at my question.

I'd never believed that praying ever achieved anything. People usually prayed when somebody was about to die or something, and not for *toothache*, surely? Would God really be interested in that guy's ridiculous toothache? I thought they might have been playing around or something.

"God is interested in the big and small things, but we may not always receive His healing. We can but ask!" said Sherry.

I supposed it made sense if you believed in God, but, to a person like me, it all seemed rather absurd.

As I walked home from the village that night, I messaged Kate.

11.13pm: "Going home to write!!! Thanks to you!"

The joy in that simple message is very clear to see. It wasn't alcohol, as the Canadians drink little, so I wasn't drunk whilst with them. My new best friend was leaving the country, and would probably be more interested in events abroad than to bother chatting to me, and yet I seemed to be thrilled and energised.

When I arrived home, despite my obvious desire to write, I didn't, because I still needed to debrief that weird day with the only one who I felt could help me.

Me, 11.47pm: "I wanted to wander off with you, as I really needed a hug at that moment. I was so emotional…"

Kate: "Why do you think you were feeling so emotional?"

Me: "It was the church at that first monastery. I'd been there before but never knew the church existed. When we went in there, I was surprised and then overwhelmed by the beauty of the architecture. Also, it wasn't like other churches with the excess of riches. It was plain and simple and perfect. Then Sherry sang out of nowhere, and it was sublime. It touched me. The acoustics were perfect… I was very quiet when we got back into the car and went to Jan's monastery. I was still emotional there and loved the place and the vision he has for it. So, I needed to hug you bad. I can't understand what happened, nor what happens when you hug me… even now the emotions come back… that place, that moment touched me in a way I can't explain…"

Kate: "You are supposed to be writing!"

Me: "Yeah, I know, but today was really special for me and I don't want to let go of it just yet…"

It's clear from this conversation, written at the end of that day, that something really special had just happened to me, and that I did not know what it was. What is clear is that I begin to use extreme adjectives (overwhelming, sublime, etc.), and I tell Kate that I want it never to end.

I slept so soundly that night.

Kate: "When we picked Dave up for his first Community Lunch, he seemed a little nervous for the day, which was understandable because he was going to meeting a lot of new people and he really didn't know what to expect. Easing the tension, we went to visit a monastery before we joined the group. This seemed to relax him since he had been there before… until we went into the sanctuary. I know how Dave felt about 'the Church' and so I understood why he was suddenly uncharacteristically quiet and tense. But he walked around and looked at things. Suddenly, a beautiful song flowed out of Sherry in worship like she couldn't contain it. Covered in goose bumps and full of awe, I wondered if Dave would feel something too and prayed again that he would. When we left, he looked practically ill and was still weirdly quiet. When we got to Community Lunch, he desperately requested a hug. Hugging is my greatest gifting, so that wasn't an odd request to me, but I could tell that he was shaken. Before long, he relaxed in the company of our community that we had brought him to meet. Basking in the hospitality and love that this group radiates, it's easy to feel comfortable. Despite his lifted mood the rest of the day, he was clearly mulling over something."

Thursday 15 July 2021

Me to Kate, 3.00pm: "I think my life will change considerably over the next, ooh, three months or so…"

This was so prophetic. I do not know where that came from, but I was clearly suddenly buzzing, even though my light and guide and new best friend had just left the country for a week. Despite only being in my life for fourteen days, we both agreed that it felt like we'd known each other for years, and yet I surprised myself by *not* missing her. She just always felt so close to me when she was away, probably because we never stopped chatting all day, every day.

Kate knew I had the habit of drinking wine whilst writing, as I normally wrote in the evenings and late into the night. I liked the taste, and it relaxed me, but, more worryingly, it was really just a bad habit of mine. I could easily drink an entire bottle of wine during a typical writing session. Before she left, she'd advised me to line up two glasses: one of wine, and the other of water. That way, I might reduce my alcohol intake by half, as well as rehydrate myself.

I gave it a go, even though I didn't think I'd be drinking the water, and I let her know I was giving it a try.

9.00pm: "Wine + water + writing: I intend to. I want to. I will. I am."

10.00pm: "I'm writing again!"

I even sent her a photo of the glasses lined up in front of my computer. Despite my doubts, after drinking the first glass of wine, I was deeply engrossed in my writing, and reached out and took a swig from the glass of water. It was only when I swallowed the contents that I looked at the glass and realised it was water. I frowned at it and continued writing. Within the next hour, I'd drunk all the water and only then went to the kitchen and refilled both glasses as before.

I did the same again and, by the time I'd finished that writing session, I'd drunk just two glasses of wine. I realised that, without the water, I'd have drunk four glasses of wine, which is basically the entire bottle. On top of that, I'd consumed the two glasses of water, which is something I rarely do.

It felt good.

Friday 16 July 2021

I slept until midday because I'd been up really late working on my old novel, which I'd abandoned months ago. As soon as I woke up, I sent Kate a message.

> *Me to Kate: "… for the first time in ages, I feel back on track. U r so recharging me. A million ETERNAL kisses for you."*

I was certainly far from unhappy, and there was absolutely no reason for this sudden surge in the joy I was visibly displaying over these next few days. I was clearly pointing the finger at Kate as being responsible, as I could see no other explanation for what was happening to me, despite her relentless advice that it wasn't her at all.

On Saturday, I went out with the Canadians, had dinner with them, and met some of their Spanish friends. I told Kate that I had had "an amazing night in the village". Afterwards, I still wrote a thousand words of my novel.

Sunday 18 July 2021

Looking back over events for this book, it became abundantly clear that this was the day something surreal, or supernatural, was undoubtedly happening to me. From the following messages, you can see that I was behaving weirdly. You might have thought that I was 'tripping' on something, yet I'd not taken any alcohol or drugs. I felt over-the-moon-happy, and, outwardly, I was acting oddly indeed!

Once I got back from a long and energising bike ride, I sent this to my friend:

> *3.00pm: "CREATIVE OVERLOAD WARNING! My brain is swimming with ideas, thoughts, stories, questions. I haven't felt like this for a long time! I need to cool it down a tad, so watching the Formula 1 race… came up with a new book idea too!"*

I had to *cool my brain down*! Seriously, something unusual was happening to me.

The new book idea that I mentioned came from the relics I'd seen in the church on that eventful day. I'd been researching who Saint Veremundo was, and I'd discovered he was the Patron Saint of Pilgrims in *Navarra*. He was famous for performing a miracle in front of hundreds of starving local people, where he was said to have fed them with the help of a flock of birds that came out of the heavens.

I was quite amazed at the discovery of these facts, as I was spending most of my days with pilgrims, and cycling or walking along the *camino* in *Navarra*. All the pilgrims drank the free wine from the font next to his monastery, which is provided in his memory, and yet few knew why – or indeed *who* he was – despite having just walked across *Navarra* – *his Navarra*! I felt like I had to do him justice, to write his story, to bring him out of the shadows and to the fore, somehow.

The name of the book came to me instantly: *Listen to the Camino*, and I decided it would be a book to help guide pilgrims on their walk, with stories of ancient history written along the route, but also of the new history that was being made every day on the way. I was discovering these stories all the time, as I met pilgrims in the café or out on the *camino*. Yes, this Veremundo fella would feature heavily in my new guidebook for the *Navarra* section of the *camino*.

At 4.00pm, I dusted off my guitar and attempted to strum a few chords, much to the delight of my puppy. I recorded her reaction as she howled next to me, and sent the video to Kate for a laugh.

I wrote to her again, clearly still buzzing – watching the F1 race wasn't cooling my brain down at all!

> Me to Kate, 5.31pm: "Oh Kate, I'm so on fire right now with creative desire. I've never felt anything so powerful as this. I don't know if it is due to the recent drought I've been through, or due to the KT effect, but I love this feeling! I know that as soon as the race finishes, I'm gonna write. But not about that yet, about how my life changed a couple of weeks ago, and of how I should have seen the message in that owl! Thank you, Kate. I am writing from my heart, from my soul, right now. It is like a river, threatening to burst its banks..."

And that comment about "writing of how my life has suddenly changed" was the birth of a second book, born just two hours after *Listen to the Camino* was thought up! I gave this second book the working title of *My Camino*, and that book eventually became this one, *Come to the Table*. Both books came to me that day, the day that I was on fire for no apparent reason. Just twenty days earlier, I had been so deeply depressed that I was in obvious danger. I couldn't see any way forward. The future had seemed very dark to me back then.

In less than three weeks, this is how I was behaving and feeling and producing work. I had swung from one extreme to the other, with the first 'lift' coming the day that Kate and I met, followed by the big 'emotion' that came just two weeks after that (four days ago).

It was on this day that I also sent a prayer emoticon for the first time in my life.

To Kate, of course.

> Kate: "I was excited to be going to Kosovo to work with the college team, but I was a little sad to be leaving Dave behind, as he was becoming interesting. He had already really changed from the unhappy man I had met two weeks ago, and we were fast becoming friends. For someone who wanted nothing to do with 'that Jesus

stuff', he was asking really good questions and letting me say what I wanted to say to him. He didn't agree and was wrestling with it all, but at least we were talking about it."

Monday 19 July 2021

This was the first day that I really started to question events happening around me and to me. The high of yesterday wasn't as strong, but it was – whatever it was – clearly still within me, and affecting me. I realised that what Kate had been insisting all of this time was true – this wasn't really coming from her at all, but that something else was at work here, something I could not, for the life of me, understand. I told her I had questions for her when she got back, and mentioned many small coincidences that had been happening since her arrival. Kate's response was just what I had expected from her.

> Kate, 11.13pm: "Haha, you call them coincidences. I don't believe in coincidences. I can go on, but you know where this is headed!"

Yeah, here we go – Jesus again!

These small coincidences I mentioned, which had been happening since the day Kate had arrived, were nothing compared to the coincidences that were about to happen to me over the next few weeks.

As expected, she promised to answer any question I had when she got back home tomorrow. And my questions were about to start really piling up.

CHAPTER 8

TRYING TO UNDERSTAND

Tuesday 20 July 2021

I drove the ninety minutes to Bilbao airport to collect Kate. She was extremely tired after a long and stressful journey, but she stayed awake for the whole trip back, just to answer my burning questions, and to help guide me with her 'infinite' wisdom.

I questioned her again about her 'supernatural' abilities, such as her wisdom, her energy, and her shiny face. She answered me as if she were telling me the sky was blue.

"It's not me, it's God. They are gifts from God. God is working through me."

I shook my head as I drove. "But I believe in the things I can see with my own eyes. I've told you, I believe in *you* because I can see *you*, and I see what *you* do. I cannot see *anything* beyond you, therefore I cannot believe in anything other than it is you."

"Dave, you're contradicting yourself. You can't believe both ways. You *see* my 'abilities' – therefore I *have* them – yet *you* can't explain them. So my explanation of them *is* correct, or I am wrong about God. Either they do come from the Lord, or I don't have them. So which is it?"

It was a valid comment, but I still would not accept her argument. I did *not* believe in Jesus. I was the last person on the planet who would believe in Jesus, or see the light, or be converted – whatever you called it. It'd seriously be a miracle if that were ever to happen to me.

Kate: "You were clearly confused about what was happening to you and around you, but you were adamant it was not God, and you kept saying things like, 'It's you, I don't believe in God', and 'I can see something, but I'm confused.' You – one hundred percent – didn't believe me."

"Look, I think you should read the Bible. Have you ever read it?" Kate asked.

I had, as a child. I'd found the stories fascinating, but they were just stories to me. Nobody believed in the Bible in my childhood home.

I thought about it. Maybe it wouldn't be a bad thing to do. As a writer, just to compare the stories, how I read them as a child, to how I might perceive them now?

"Okay. I'll get one and try to read it."

Clearly, I was justifying why I would now read the Bible – avoiding any hint of anything other than 'researching' it as a story-teller, and not promising that I would actually pick it up and begin reading.

Kate offered me her Bible, but I refused, as I felt it was a treasured possession to her. Imagine if my puppy ate it?

Wednesday 21 July 2021

It had been just three weeks since Kate had first arrived in my Spanish village, yet something seemed to have messed with my mind's internal clock. So much had happened to me over these three short weeks that it felt much longer, and Kate's friendship felt eternal.

Something new also began happening to me from this day: I started to wake up super-early for a change. This day I woke up at 8.00am, later days at 7.00am. This was just so unnatural for me. I had always been a late riser – how many times had I been late for school?

Fortunately, it was Wednesday, which meant Community Lunch day!

Kate and the Canadians picked me up. Kate was excited to meet up with the friends she'd made there on her previous visits.

On arrival at the old monastery, we opened the doors and windows to let in fresh air. It had been closed up for a while, and the atmosphere was quite stale. We soon spotted a couple of wild birds that had somehow found their way into the monastery. We tried to get them out by forming human walls with hands raised, but they were very stressed and panicky. I think they'd been trapped inside for a day or two and were disorientated, hungry, and thirsty.

We got them to a passageway with enormous windows, and one poor bird kept flying into the glass to escape. We tried to usher it down to the large double doors at the end of the passage, but it kept flying into the invisible glass. I was worried it was going to hurt itself.

We eventually got it close to the open doors, but it flew straight past them, slammed into another window, and slid down to the ledge at the bottom. It sat there, panting.

I was standing next to it, and I could see it had little strength left. Instinctively, I reached down to it with my hand, and, to my surprise, it hopped straight onto my finger. I raised my hand, turned around, and walked out into the garden. The bird sensed it was free and flew away.

People called me Bird Whisperer for the rest of the afternoon, and I was quietly impressed and amazed at what had just taken place. That had never happened before in my life.

Kate just said, "Somebody is trying to tell you something!"

Over the next seven days, I got into a new routine of waking early, going for a ride along the *camino*, meeting pilgrims, even inviting some camping pilgrims to camp in my garden. I did lots of writing, and spent as much time as I could with Kate before she went abroad again, and hung out at the Oasis, enjoying the vibe.

Saturday 24 July 2021

"I'm on fire with this book guide!"

I was writing three books simultaneously: my original novel called *The Listening Room*, the new pilgrims' guide called *Listen to the Camino*, and my new life story, *Come to the Table*.

Wednesday 28 July 2021

A week later, whilst talking to Jan at the Community Lunch, I suddenly offered to donate all the profits I make from *Listen to the Camino* to the monastery they were refurbishing. I don't know why, but I felt I had to.

Kate was away again, this time in the UK. She was spending three weeks working in Birmingham, Scotland, and London, then visiting a refugee centre in Greece for a week. I'd have preferred her to stay around, as I knew I was processing *something*, and I genuinely needed her help. Also, the café was going to close for holidays next week, and the Canadians were going away. I'd be all on my own, and I was worried about it. However, Kate and I never stopped chatting whenever she was out of the country. It was as if she never left, and she was always a comfort for me in those weird times.

I spent the afternoon travelling around the locations connected with Saint Veremundo, researching material for the book, and discovering stories from pilgrims passing through.

Thursday 29 July 2021

In my texts to Kate, I could see a calmer me emerging from the initial fervour of the emotion I'd felt from that original church visit. It seemed to have matured, and was under more control, although it did sometimes surge.

> Me to Kate: *"You brought me back. Gave me a love of life. Of people. Animated me. Saved me. I could go on, but a million thanks. I feel so good these days. A purpose again. A direction. All because of you."*

I was still pointing the finger at Kate for what was happening, as I couldn't see any other explanation that made any sense to me.

> *"I am the complete opposite of what I was in the weeks before your arrival. From rock bottom to sky high in such a short time.*

Sometimes I have to stop and switch it off as it is quite… not overwhelming, not really tiring… dizzying?"

Kate simply replied that she couldn't take the credit for that, and, as always, she deflected my opinions to Jesus.

I still couldn't find adequate words to describe the feeling that had been in me for the past two weeks, and noted that sometimes it surged of its own accord.

I was also, for the first time in my life, quite comfortable showing people my writings, even at the first draft. I had never done this before, and had let nobody read anything I wrote, not until it was fully polished and ready for publishing.

As I walked home from the village at 2.00pm, I saw a huge eagle. It was on the arm of the man I'd seen with the owl on the day I met Kate, three weeks earlier. I petted the bird and smiled, wondering if this was yet another message for me.

Later that evening, as I sat outside the Oasis having a wine with Nath, a local guy came up to us. I knew of him as he had a lovely little puppy that I always played with. With him was a guy I'd never seen before: Ed, an Irish man. Ed was quickly to become an integral part of my life.

Oh, and Ed was a believer, just like everybody who was coming into my life of late.

Saturday 31 July 2021

Mark was a teacher I'd employed when I was running the language academy with my ex. We'd connected well, and he hadn't forgotten me when he organised his farewell party. It was in *Logroño*, a city just fifteen minutes' drive away, but it was to be in two parts. First, we were to meet at a private venue in the city for lunch, then in the evening we were meeting at a military sports and social complex. It was the evening event that would stay in my mind due to what happened there.

It had been just ten days since I first held a wild bird in my hand at the monastery. At Mark's party, as I stood in the gardens, talking to a man who had a lot of hair, I watched as a small bird flew out of the tree behind him, and landed straight on his head, in his hair! I couldn't believe it – it was so unexpected.

The guy felt it land and panicked, not knowing what it was. He reached up to smack whatever it was out of his hair. I reacted quickly and stopped him. The bird was entangled in his hair, and couldn't break free, so I put my hand up to it and – you guessed it – it stepped onto my finger, and let me rescue it too.

The bird just sat there, chilled and calm, looking at me. I reached for my phone, fired up the camera, and took two pictures of it, albeit not very well-focused, before the bird casually flew away to freedom. I was so pleased to have proof that this was really happening.

"Wow!" said the man. "Bird Whisperer!"

I posted the picture on *Instagram* and wrote:

> *"This is the second time in two weeks that I have been privileged to have a wild bird sit on my hand and trust me. WTF is happening here???"*

The second bird to step onto my finger

Kate's response to this latest drama made me giggle:

> *"Did that little bird just land on your hand like you're freaking Snow White or something..?"*

As July drew to a close and a new month began, my thinking changed too. I began reflecting a lot on my life, and writing thoughts and feelings down. My life seemed to take off of its own accord, and I was becoming a mere passenger, sitting back, observing events as they unfolded, taking notes, and learning to live with, and accept, that ever-present emotion in my chest.

The coming month of August was to be another weird period in my weird story, but one full of discovery. It was only then that I accepted some answers to what was really happening to me – and to what that sublime emotion inside of me really was.

CHAPTER 9

DISCOVERING

Wednesday 4 August 2021

The first Wednesday of the month saw me go to Community Lunch, this time taking Nath along with me for her first visit. As expected, everybody fell in love with her, and she loved everybody in return. As she played football with the kids, I sat and chatted to a few of the people there who were now becoming good friends.

We spoke of the French guy who'd had the toothache. He had originally been looking for answers whilst walking the *camino*, but when he stayed at the *albergue* run by Oasis Trails, he felt drawn to the place and volunteered to work at the *albergue*. During his time with the team, he accepted Jesus into his heart, and was subsequently baptised in a nearby river.

I was curious to see what all of that really meant, so they graciously gave me a copy of the interview he gave before he'd left for home.

I wasn't sure it would help me answer any of my questions. It was more out of curiosity to see what had happened to him, and what had made him want to walk into a river whilst there. I stored it on my phone with a view to watching it at some point.

The thing was, my situation differed from his. I had never gone looking for God like he had. I wasn't searching for answers, hadn't been witness to a supernatural event, as everybody else I was meeting seemed to have been. The idea of a single, intelligent God was not something I believed in. It was just too fantastical to believe.

Thursday 5 August 2021

During a chat with Kate, she casually told me she was praying for me. This was my response:

> *"… for the first time in my life, I appreciate somebody praying for me. Thank you."*

I didn't believe in the power of prayer, but if somebody with Kate's 'abilities' was going to pray for me, what harm could it do?

I later learned that so many people in countries all over the world were praying for me. Kate had been praying for me before she had met me. All of Kate's contacts, many churches in the US, in Canada, people from all over Europe, in the home countries of this large, extended family of believers who were actually fully informed of me, were all praying that I would see the light. I was on a prayer list of many, one that had been growing exponentially since Wes and Sherry had first prayed for me back in January. And, by July, my life had filled up with Christians, all of whom began repeatedly praying for me, and asking others to do the same.

I was on a prayer hit list.

I've since heard of other people who had been placed on such a hit list, and have had their lives similarly changed.

Friday 6 August 2021

Ed had agreed to help me out in my sizeable garden for a week or two. It was too big for me to handle alone, and had been completely neglected through my long months of depression. It seriously needed a lot of loving care. He was available and itching to be gainfully employed, so we agreed on a deal, and he came over that Friday and began working with me. He was to come daily, and spend a lot of time at my home. After working through the heat of the day, we'd usually end it with home-made food and cold beers.

Rasta, one of my three dogs, supervising Ed working in my garden

The result was a much happier garden, a puppy that finally accepted her first stranger as a friend, and a new friendship for me (another Christian, naturally).

That night I watched the French guy's interview. I was very curious about how he described what happened to him when he finally accepted Jesus into his heart. I replayed his words repeatedly. Incredibly, what he was describing, with amazing accuracy and total conviction, was almost identical to the internal emotion that I was feeling, and had been feeling since it first came over me in that church. He called it 'The Holy Spirit'.

Kate had been speaking to me constantly about such things for the past four weeks, but I was unwilling to accept her view of the world.

I'd heard of the Holy Spirit, of course, but had never grasped it. The Spirit always seemed to be something of an unknown element of Christianity to many people, me included. I had a good idea of what God was supposed to be, and I believed in Jesus as a man who lived and preached good stuff, whether or not He was the Son of God. But a Spirit?

"In the name of the Father, the Son, and the Holy Ghost, Amen."

So, what was this *ghost* thing all about, anyway? How could there be a spirit involved in all of this? To understand what was happening to me, I needed to know what it was. I was also desperately in need of an alternative explanation for what was occurring. I would accept any evidence to disprove God, and yet everything I was hearing was completely contrary to what I believed.

I went online and researched the Holy Spirit that night. The first thing I discovered was, it is not an *it*, but a *He*. Jesus sent Him into the Apostles to give them skills and abilities – or *gifts* – to help them do what they were about to do, once Jesus finally ascended to heaven.

I recalled Kate's use of the word *gifts* to describe her abilities, as we had driven back from the airport. *So this is what she was talking about?* I delved in deeper.

The Holy Spirit is said to be God and Jesus, and is supposed to be found in people! Three in one – the Trinity.

God in people. God in *me?* That was kind of hard to grasp, if not a little weird, so I read on. This was to be a eureka moment for me. In fact, it was quite mind-blowing.

I discovered the term 'Fruits of the Holy Spirit', which is something I had never heard of before, but had actually unknowingly witnessed many times, with my very own eyes. I realised instantly that these 'fruits' clearly explained all of those shiny faces I had recently encountered!

Kate and the others at the community suddenly 'made sense' to me. It answered all of my questions and doubts and confusion about the shiny-faced people I'd been meeting, and made their abilities absolutely real and clear and truthful. Their faces shone, and this was the only explanation I could find of their inner energy, their glow – it was just as Kate had been telling me all along!

What is supposed to happen – and what the French guy said happened to him – is that when you repent and invite Jesus into your heart, Jesus will accept you without question. He'll then fill you with the Holy Spirit, and with the Holy Spirit comes the Fruits of the Spirit.

If you do that, and do it from your heart, you apparently get these:

❖ *love* ❖ *joy* ❖ *peace* ❖ *patience*
❖ *kindness* ❖ *generosity* ❖ *faithfulness*
❖ *gentleness* ❖ *self-control*

It must be the most welcome parcel anybody could ever hope to receive! I thought of all the new people that had come into my life this year – they all had these attributes in abundance. It was undeniable in all of them. That is why Nath and I felt so safe and loved and at peace amongst them.

Also, I couldn't deny that I had been feeling so much of these in myself in the last few weeks. I was certainly overjoyed, felt totally at peace with everything, and had certainly become more patient with people like my irritating neighbour. I'd always been quite generous, but as Kate later told her colleague: "Dave is one of the most generous people you will ever meet."

Some of these fruits had never been a part of my life until that incident in the church, especially joy, peace, and self-control. Now they were so much a part of me. As for the others, they had either seriously increased in me since that day, or had at least increased enough for me – and others – to see.

But there was more to come.

One of the Spirit's many roles is to make you more like Jesus, to mould you and guide you, and to reveal to you the areas of your life that you can change or improve on.

The Spirit can also give you incredible abilities, which are called 'Gifts of the Spirit' and these gifts are the most generous gifts any person could receive.

You don't always get them, and you probably won't get them all, but the Spirit endows you with the gifts you will need, according to whatever God has planned for you.

I've always lived by the mantra that 'if something seems to be too good to be true, then it probably is…' and, a few months ago, I'd have said all of this was ancient hocus-pocus. But the evidence of my own eyes, and my personal feelings, and experiences of late, were telling me that there must be some truth to this! How else could all of this, written thousands of years ago, be describing me now, and also those around me?

I read on, scanning through the list of the seven Gifts of the Holy Spirit, and was blown away:

❖ *wisdom* ❖ *knowledge* ❖ *healing*

❖ *miracles* ❖ *prophecy*

❖ *discernment* ❖ *speaking in tongues*

The Spirit can give you some or all of these abilities! It instantly clarified all the questions I had of Kate and the others! Her wisdom, discernment, even her healing ability!

It made little sense, and yet it made everything clear to me. I sat back in my chair and stared at the screen, thinking hard.

So, was that really it? Was the Holy Spirit – *God*! – actually inside of *me*? Was that what had entered me in that church three weeks ago? It seemed absurd to me, yet it supported everything Kate had been constantly telling – and yelling – at me.

If it *were* true, it would basically mean that for the whole 55 years of my life, I had been completely wrong. Had I spent the whole of my life completely blind to the actual truth? Had my life been pointless to date?

I focused in on that emotion within me. I could only describe it as *an emotion* as I had absolutely no point of reference for it – I had felt nothing like it before in my whole life.

I had to admit that the feeling was most definitely not anything physical, and it felt like it was on a spiritual level, although I did not know what a 'spiritual level' was! Whatever was inside of me was just beyond any words I could come up with – and I'm a writer!

This feeling was clearly pleasurable for me. It was the most beautiful feeling I have ever felt. In fact, as a pleasure, it was way off the scale, and it was very hard to nail down.

Also, it wasn't at a constant 'level', yet it hadn't continued to grow from day one, as the French guy's had. Mine was very strong on day one, so much so that it floored me, rendered me speechless, then surged so much in the weeks that followed that I might have looked and behaved like I was tripping on illegal drugs, and then it settled down somewhat. But it still surged occasionally, just as it was doing right then, as I was discovering these answers to my many questions.

I sat in silence, stunned. *This simply cannot be real?* But then, it 'solved' all of those people around me. There was simply no plausible alternative for Kate's wisdom, or why these guys had a glow to them – shiny faces – which I saw in all of them, including that vicar that worked for me, all those years ago.

It all fitted. It all fell instantly into place.

> *"Those who look to Him are radiant, their faces are never covered in shame."*   – Psalms 34:5

At that moment, I needed two things: a strong drink, and somebody wise who could help me process this information.

> Me, 11.53pm: *"This explains you so much. I can see no other explanation than that which you tell me."*
>
> Kate: *"I've been telling you this the whole time.* 😄 *It's the Holy Spirit, dude."*
>
> Me: *"And the Fruit of the Holy Spirit also explains you, and others…"*
>
> Kate: *"You're getting it!"*
>
> Me, 12.07am: *"I find the things that are happening to me, and the understanding of why they might be happening (as nothing else is available to explain them) very tiring… is that normal?… I mean, I feel very sleepy, more than normal. And my dreams are so detailed, just like my stories."*
>
> Kate: *"I think maybe when people are so used to not knowing the truth and living in this bubble of non-understanding, when you*

start to know the truth, and the extent to which you are loved by God, the weight of everything can be quite exhausting."

Me: *"As always, I cannot argue with what you say."*

That weekend most definitely turned out to be an epiphany for me.

Sunday 8 August, 4.47pm:
"I'm beginning to feel that something is happening, that I'm being saved. I felt magical the other week, totally on another level in my head. I was floating and writing… never felt that 'high' before, and I know if I can get there and stay there, I can write beautifully."

I then discussed Ed with Kate:

Me: *"I mean, he's even telling me how to find God, to call out to Him!!!! It's as though it was meant to happen that day in the monastery with you, but I'm too resistant, too hard, and I just had 'inexplicable emotions', so Ed is here with specific instructions…"*

Kate: *"God always gives us what we need and gives us the grace to meet us where we are."*

Me: *"I think the reason I am so tired of late is because of the intense conflict raging inside of me. The old me is saying stuff like (and I'll use a word I just read in an [reader of my book] email to me), 'don't pay attention to such TOSH…' whilst the new me is saying, 'but come on! Can you explain what is happening to me here and now? Since Kate arrived? There is absolutely NO explanation available to me, yet there is one being given to me! So what do you believe, nothing? Or the only explanation available?'"*

I then said that that had just led to another ton of questions, and I wished Kate were there with me, to sit and talk it all out in person.

"And (please don't tell anyone) – I just questioned God directly, aloud… for the first time in my life."

Kate then gently told me of a course that was perfect for somebody in my situation. It was called the Alpha course, and it might help me understand what was happening, and give me some answers. She did this tactfully because I was still very skeptical of it all. I agreed to give it a try, and she informed me that the Canadians would set one up in the village that I could attend.

That night, I watched the French guy's interview once again. He'd given himself through his belief that God existed, then clearly described feeling the Holy Spirit within him, growing and filling him. Our feelings were so clearly similar, and yet we had never spoken to each other about those feelings or experiences. In fact, the first time I met him was at my first Community Lunch, on the day that I first felt that feeling, and we hadn't even spoken then. How could he have been describing the same feelings I had, if it were all made up? We both felt the same thing, but individually.

I did more Googling to see what other people 'felt' when they received the Spirit, but most people felt it in different ways. It just seems very coincidental that the two of us had had an extremely similar experience.

And then I spotted a problem in all of this: he *believed*, then he gave himself, then he felt the Spirit.

I certainly didn't believe, I hadn't given myself, and yet I felt the Spirit strongly.

So how could it be the same thing? And was it possible for the Holy Spirit to enter me in this way? *Without an invitation*? According to everything I was hearing, and everything I was reading, the Spirit only comes to those who give themselves to Him first, and *not* beforehand.

I needed a definitive answer to this, as it was all unfamiliar territory for me, so I asked Kate this fundamental question. Her response:

"Who are we to set parameters for what God can or cannot do?"

Fair point, and it made perfect sense to me. If God were the creator of everything, omnipresent, all seeing, and all-powerful, then who are we, us mere mortals, to say what He can or can't do, regardless of how we interpret the Bible? Maybe *man* deciding on *God's* abilities was where religion had gone so drastically wrong?

> *"God's power is unlimited. He needs no teachers to guide or correct Him. Others have praised God for what He has done, so join with them."* — Job 36:22-24

And that emotion – or entity? – I still clearly felt inside of me. And that it wasn't static – that it surged when, for example, I was discovering the information regarding the Fruits of the Holy Spirit, made it feel alive. It was as if it were happy with me for finding those answers, as if it were trying to communicate with me: *Good boy! Keep up the good work!*

The feeling was also becoming addictive. I grew to love the surges, and the surges came when I was discovering 'the truth', as Kate would put it, or even when I was in the company of certain people praying near me, such as at the Community Lunch.

In search of the truth, I revisited the church where it had all started, and sat in silence with Saint Veremundo. There was another woman in there, deep in prayer, and I felt a little foolish, awkward even. Had she not been there, I might have even tried talking to the saint. I felt like an imposter.

I was after answers, of course. I don't know what I was hoping for, but I left there after an hour, quite dissatisfied that nothing had 'happened'.

As Kate later said: "It is not place-driven – it can happen anywhere."

Meanwhile, Ed was with me every day, working in the garden, playing with the dogs, and eating and drinking. All the time he was counselling me: "Ask Him aloud, just talk to the Big Man."

It was as if he had been sent as backup, or with a different approach, to help get me to see the light.

I spoke to Kate regarding this, and this was her response:

> *"I have been quite blunt with you, as He told me that was the best approach for you."*

I cannot deny that this advice was spot on: I'm seriously no good at hints and intimations.

My Camino (the early version of this book)

In this first week of August, I wrote the following in the story that eventually became this book:

> *"I am now five weeks into my new journey – my new life – five weeks from that old me, and not only do I not know how long this one will last, but I have absolutely no idea where it will end. This story is, as yet, unwritten. All that I know is that this is better than any journey I have ever been on in my life, and not knowing where it will lead to is part of the pleasure.*
>
> *Taking off in a plane whilst my instructor waved at me from the safety of the taxiway was possibly the most terrifying thing I have done in my life. Landing that plane solo – and surviving – was undoubtably the most amazing feeling I have ever felt in my first life.*
>
> *My second life – my new journey – is only five weeks old, yet every day of my new life always brings me joy. I now smile at strangers, ask after them, and even hug them. People respond to me in the same, positive way. Complete strangers now become total friends.*
>
> *In these last five weeks, I have had an experience far greater than the feeling of not dying in my first ever solo aircraft landing. What gave me this massive high? To be honest, I cannot put my finger on it. All I know is that it was something to do with feeling good to be alive, blessed to be loved, and that, for the first time, I felt there was a purpose to my existence.*
>
> *I feel reborn. Am I there yet? Oh no, I most certainly am not.*
>
> *In fact, all that I do know is that I am far from it…*

CHAPTER 10

TRANSFORMATION

Wednesday 6 August 2021

Whilst sitting outside the Oasis with Nath, we bumped into a couple of pilgrims we'd met the day before at the *albergue* in *Villamayor*. One guy was very brash, bristling with energy, and determined to complete the *camino* as fast as he could. I felt he was rather missing the point of the pilgrimage.

"Can I give you some advice?" I said to him. "Slow down a bit, and maybe stop, and *listen to the camino…*"

His chin instantly dropped to his chest, and his shoulders drooped. It was very clear to me that my words had just had some kind of impact on him, and I wasn't sure why. I initially feared that he might have taken offence.

After a few seconds in that position, he looked up at me. "Do you know what just happened to me, dude? Not more than fifteen minutes ago?"

I shook my head.

"I was washing my clothes in the sink, and listening to a podcast, and my AirPods fell out of my ears straight into the water. Not one, but both of them. Ruined them completely. I now have no headphones to listen to music or podcasts whilst on the *camino*, as I always do. That just happened, just now…"

It was just another coincidence.

"Okay, so just take a day or two, walking the *camino* without the headphones. Listen to the silence, listen to the people, *talk* to the people. But above all, just listen – listen to the *camino*. Why don't you try it, now that you have no headphones?"

"Oh man, yeah. I'll do it. I'll definitely do it…"

Thursday 7 August 2021

I found something in my bathroom that I'd never seen before. It was a small book, placed on the side as if somebody had been reading it whilst using the throne. It was called *Living Water*[4]: a tiny book aimed at non-believers, helping to guide them towards God. None of my friends claimed ownership or knowledge of it, and I had no idea how it had come to be in my bathroom.

Friday 8 August 2021

Me to Kate: "… I'm in a good place. In fact, I've never felt so alive."

That weekend, I spoke to Kate about the mysterious appearance of that book, and also of some of my worries regarding Nath and her busy social life.

Sunday 15 August 2021

Me: "Pray for her please… I also 'pray' for her, at night, when I go to bed."

Despite not being a believer, here I was asking Kate to pray for Nath, therefore believing in the power of her prayer, and admitting to actually praying for her myself, although the scare quotes indicate I wasn't totally sure that that was what I was doing!

Kate and I have a very compatible sense of humour. Throughout most of our exchanges, there were laughter emoticons, such as this:

> *Me: "I finished reading that book, Living Waters. I found it really interesting… I want to read more… I want to read the whole Bible now, for sure, starting at the beginning, but it is a bit like Star Wars though. What is the beginning?"*

Kate: "It's called Genesis, and it literally starts with, 'In the beginning..." 😄

The origin of that book is still unknown, but it gave me a desire to read the Bible.

Me: "I feel you are the key to this path I am walking..."

Kate: "I'm not the key. Jesus is the key. It's His book."

Wednesday 18 August 2021

I met a complete stranger at this Community Lunch, who told me straightaway that I had "a beautiful face, and a beautiful soul". His wife subsequently told Nath she was "so handsome". Nath had never been called handsome before, ever. On the day Nath gets called handsome for the first time, I get called beautiful. Translation errors, clearly, but I marvelled at that coincidence of Nath and I both being described with crossed-gender adjectives like that.

The following week, I met this couple for a second time at Community Lunch. The guy gave me a bear hug, and, as he did so, I felt a large crack in my ribs. Once he released me, I looked down and discovered my sunglasses, which had been hanging off my t-shirt collar, had snapped. I was quite relieved it wasn't a rib. I had them repaired, only to repeat the same error at the third lunch, with the same guy, who gave me a tremendous hug again.

Wes publicly thanked me for bringing Nath into their lives, with 'her beautiful smile that lights up a room'. She was so touched, as was I.

Whilst there, we met two pilgrims from the US, Karen[5] and Rachel, walking together. Rachel had apparently fasted for five days to get some guidance from God prior to her pilgrimage, and "all she got was Karen".

We met up with them the following day in *Viana* and had dinner with them. Karen enthralled us all with her beautiful way of talking about her faith. They told me that my "veil was being lifted", and read me – and sent me – a verse from the Bible:

"But whenever someone turns to the Lord, the veil is taken away. For the Lord is the Spirit, and wherever the Spirit of the Lord is, there is freedom. So all of us who have had that veil removed can see and reflect the glory of the Lord. And the Lord – who is the Spirit – makes us more and more like Him, as we are changed into His glorious image." — 2 Corinthians:16-18

I read that passage many times, and saw again references to shiny people in it. It also stated that people are made more and more like Jesus. I was undeniably a much happier, friendlier, and calmer person than I had ever been at any time in my life, and I didn't know what the reason behind these changes was. I was undoubtedly changing – or rather – being changed, but I still didn't think that I was what the passage described – someone who was turning to the Lord – but nor could I explain exactly where the changes were coming from.

Friday 20 August 2021

Kate arrived in Greece yesterday. She was staying there for a week before returning to Spain. After a brief chat with her, she said this:

"It brings so much joy to my heart to see you transforming on this journey of God's truth. You are already so different from the person I first met, and I'm so excited about what God is doing in you and through you."

The change in me had been, truthfully, quite spectacular. I was unrecognisable from the guy she had met just *seven* weeks before. I don't just mean in how I felt, but in how others perceived me. Local people in the village said that I glowed, or they "sensed an energy from me", as they did from Kate or Wes and Sherry. And then there were the complete strangers, people who had never met me before, saying similar things.

I've since discovered many other passages in the Bible which clearly reference this. The 'secret to life' glow that I had detected in the vicar years ago, and was seeing in so many new friends in my new life, was apparently evidence of the Holy Spirit living in the individual person. We see the Holy Spirit in people, and I was witnessing it in others. I later found out that not everybody is aware of this glow, or is perhaps unwilling to see it. Many talk of 'an energy', or an aura, or a feeling of peace in some people. Those that do not believe in God are often not willing to admit that they are witnessing *Him* in person, or just don't realise that that is *who* they are seeing.

The previous seven weeks had certainly been a surreal experience for that dedicated atheist of many, many years.

Tuesday 24 August 2021

I share a long driveway with my neighbour, who I have had ongoing problems with for most of the time I have lived here. She hasn't spoken to me in about eighteen months, despite the proximity of our homes. She also completely ignores *anybody* associated with my house.

A few nights previously, I had had a dream about her. I dreamed I was working on the driveway cutting my hedgerow, when she walked down to me and said hi, and told me it was too cold to be cutting the hedgerow. I responded, and we hugged, and everything was okay with the world. In the dream, that spot was just ten metres from our shared, gated entrance, along a one hundred metre driveway. I'd told Ed about the dream that morning.

He came to the house as usual on Tuesday, and we decided to cut the hedgerow along the driveway, as the growth was reducing the width of the drive. We spent an hour steadily working our way down the driveway. He was cutting, and I was collecting and disposing of the dropped foliage. I had no idea what my neighbour was up to that day, and I cared even less.

Approximately ten metres from the gate, at the exact spot in the dream, I picked up a pile of branches and carried them around into my garden to dispose of them. When I came back, I spotted my neighbour exiting the driveway on foot, having just passed Ed.

I asked him if he had had any problems with her. He told me that as she had passed he'd smiled and said hello to her, and *she smiled back and spoke politely to him.*

It wasn't exactly what had happened in the dream, but it was uncomfortably too close to be a coincidence.

> 6.52pm: *"My life was normal, dull, and routine. Now, it is super-weird… and amazing!"*

Sunday 29 August 2021

Kate returned to *Viana* today and met Ed for the first time at the café. Prior to her arrival, I'd taken a very long and invigorating bike ride up the *camino*, speaking to many pilgrims. I told one of them about the book I was writing (this one), and she wanted to know when it would be finished.

I replied, "So do I!"

Monday 30 August 2021

This day was a tough day for my family and me. It was the birthday of my deceased brother, Paul, and it was the first one without him. It was always easy for me to remember Paul's birthday, as his was just two days prior to mine.

In the evening, I went to the Canadians' home for the very first part of the promised Alpha course. Kate gave me my birthday present – my first Bible. She had taken so much care to highlight and annotate passages she thought were important throughout the *entire* book. She really wanted me to learn from it. I was so moved.

Kate later asked me if I'd liked the course.

> 11.41pm: *"I did. It's a very slick production, with some interesting characters and views expressed. Quite thought-provoking… I think it is going to help me focus on 'events' happening around me."*

Later that night, I heard from my friend Mark. He had had a sudden illness in his family. He asked me to pray for that person. I promised him I would, and I also asked Kate if she would pray for him too. Being new to all this, I had to ask her something.

"So, what information do you need, exactly? His name, address…?"

Kate: "I think God knows who you mean."

I'm a very sarcastic person, and I loved it that Kate could match me with sarcasm.

That I was now asking Kate to pray for friends showed how far I had come in such a short time. Just six weeks ago, I'd been bewildered by prayers for a guy's toothache, thinking it was some kind of joke! Now I was asking Kate to pray for a miracle for my friend.

Kate promised me she would pray for him, and told *me* to pray for him too.

"I will. Thank you for doing that. I actually pray every day now (or am I practising…?????)"

Kate: "I know God is happy to hear from you… Don't forget to take turns, and give Him space to speak as well."

Me: "Wow, yeah. You are so wise. I'd love to hear from Him."

Tuesday 31 August

This was the day I started to read the Bible given to me by Kate. Bizarrely, I woke up at 7.00am to do so! Kate and I immediately started chatting, and, before long, our conversation turned to tomorrow's Community Lunch. I told her it was the highlight of my week because it seemed to energise me for the entire week ahead. She asked me if I knew why. I thought about it for a few seconds.

"Concentrated Jesus…?"

Kate: "Bingo!"

Later that day, I discussed my feelings again, or rather, I spoke of the 'energy' that had taken up residence inside of me for the past six weeks.

Me: "I feel the energy (or Him) rolling around me like waves. Sometimes it feels overpowering and makes me emotional… some people emit the energy so much, none more so than you. And it is getting stronger all the time for me."

Kate: "It's not an energy. It's the Holy Spirit."

Me: "I never understood what that was. I got Jesus, and God, but never thought there was a ghost too. Now I know what it is. Is that what I feel?"

This is where I finally show signs of an acceptance for what that unique feeling within me actually was, although I was still getting confused regarding how to refer to Him.

Me: "And the closer I get to Him, the stronger that becomes?"

The feeling surged whenever I was involved in what I termed *Godly stuff*, such as when somebody prayed near me, or over me, or when I was coming up with answers that mirrored Kate's.

Kate: "Yes, when you ask Jesus into your heart and into your life, the Holy Spirit comes in you and helps you."

That night I looked up a song I had heard at the Alpha course on Monday. It was to be the first of many contemporary Christian worship songs that I would add to a new playlist. What had caught my attention was that this song contained some lyrics from a song I recalled from my childhood: *Amazing Grace*, my late father's favourite song.

Broken Vessels (Amazing Grace)[6] is a beautiful tune, containing a verse from *Amazing Grace* spliced into it. It is sung by a group I soon came to love: *Hillsong Worship*.

Every time I listen to it, the Spirit inside of me surges.

Despite not being religious, my dad adored *Amazing Grace*, but I didn't know which of the many versions he liked. I texted my mum, and she surprised me by responding instantly: *Judy Collins*[7]. It amazed me that my elderly mother could instantly remember the name of the singer from so long ago.

I listened to my father's song, and the lyrics instantly struck me. Like most things during this time, the song seemed to address me directly.

That night, I asked to meet Kate, and we sat on a bench in the park near to her house. I needed to ask her more questions, and one thing that was really bugging me was the fact that people kept telling me I 'shone', and yet I did not believe in God. So, how was that possible?

She didn't need time to think about the answer, and responded immediately.

"It's like I am a window between you and God. God's light is shining through me and onto you. You are like a mirror, and some of that light bounces off you, and some people see that."

"Wow," I replied. "What a perfect analogy. Did you learn that at Bible School or something?"

"No, I didn't go to Bible School! It just came to me when you asked me the question. It's the Holy Spirit speaking, not me."

Her answers always silenced me – they were just impossible to argue with or refute. And then she said something I thought nobody would ever suggest I do.

"You should come to church with us on Sunday."

Kate: "Dave is just so full of questions about God and salvation and the work of the Holy Spirit. He's so eager for answers, even though he pretends not to believe in the ones I give him. He was so desperate tonight that I had to meet him and we talked for a couple of hours about all the things he's experiencing and how, even though he believes he is right, he has no answers. It's frustrating, because he tells me all the time that he doesn't believe, but he accepts my answers as some sort of truth.

Either I'm right about this or I'm crazy, but it's nothing in between."

Amazing Grace

Amazing grace! (how sweet the sound)
That sav'd a wretch like me!
I once was lost, but now am found,
Was blind, but now I see.

'Twas grace that taught my heart to fear,
And grace my fears reliev'd;
How precious did that grace appear?
The hour I first believ'd!

Thro' many dangers, toils, and snares,
I have already come;
'Tis grace hath brought me safe thus far,
And grace will lead me home.

The Lord has promis'd good to me,
His word my hope secures;
He will my shield and portion be
As long as life endures.

Yes, when this flesh and heart shall fail,
And mortal life shall cease;
I shall possess, within the veil,
A life of joy and peace.

The earth shall soon dissolve like snow,
The sun forbear to shine;
But God, who call'd me here below,
Will be forever mine.

John Newton, Olney Hymns, 1779

PAGE 101

[4] Living Water (The Gospel of John, with notes) by Logos 21.

PAGE 102

[5] Not her real name.

PAGE 107

[6] Broken Vessels (Amazing Grace):
Performed by Hillsong Worship.
Written by Joel Houston and Jonas Myrin.
Produced by Michael Guy Chislett.
Source: Hillsong Music and Resources LLC.

PAGE 107

[7] Amazing Grace:
Performed by Judy Collins.
Written by Judy Collins/traditional.
Produced by Mark Abramson.
Source: Elektra Records.

CHAPTER 11

SET FREE

September 2021

This was the month when things really moved along for me, and I finally began to actually 'get it'. I think it was a combination of the Alpha course, which turned out to be very informative, as well as the teachings of the Bible at the church sessions I attended. Together they helped to break down any suspicions I had of the book, and what was written in it, and its authenticity. I also read a book recommended to me by the Canadians: *The Case for Christ*[8] by Lee Strobel. The author was an atheist, an investigative journalist, and a lawyer. He set out to prove that Christ was actually a fallacy, following the decision by his wife to give herself to Jesus. He really felt that he was 'losing her' to God.

The investigation and discoveries were really in-depth, and, as an ex-police officer, I really enjoyed this book for its forensic approach. The results of his investigation left me stunned, and the ending of his story blew me away.

And of course, on top of all of this, there was Kate, and her unwavering, faultless advice, and support.

Wednesday 1 September 2021

My birthday! For weeks, I'd been telling everybody I'd be fifty-seven years of age today.

Kate knew something was amiss, and, after a quick mental calculation, she soon corrected me.

"If you were born in 1965, you're going to be fifty-six, not fifty-seven."

I didn't dare argue with her, especially when it came to maths, and I was extremely pleased not to be another year older on my birthday. I'd be fifty-six again!

We all went to Community Lunch as usual, and prayers were said over me to help me to 'see the light'. Whenever anybody prayed over me like this, I felt a wave of peace fall across me like a gentle silk blanket. It's hard to explain – you really have to experience it for yourself.

Sunday 5 September 2021

My first day at church. Kate had been very careful with me when she'd originally suggested I go to church. First, she confirmed it wasn't actually *in* a church. This pleased me for obvious reasons, yet it also left me confused.

"*We* are the church, *not* the building. God is right next to you right now, as much as He is in any church. Sometimes, we have church in a meadow at the side of a river."

I still had my church hostility, so I was very relieved not to have to walk into a stuffy, musty old building again. Kate had sensed my suspicions and had continuously softened me up.

"It's just like going to the Community Lunch, with more or less the same people, except with some songs, a few more prayers, and talking about the Bible."

The comparison to the lunch was clearly a bit of a carrot, but I'd decided to go as soon as she had suggested it a few days earlier. It just seemed right, even though I felt weird about going to church. And, of course, if Kate advised me to do it, then it'd be the right thing to do – I'd given up challenging anything she said by this point.

I just hoped nobody would find out.

Church was at the Oasis Trails monastery, and it was unlike anything I'd experienced at any church in my life. First, it was all friendly and relaxed. We sat around and had a home-made cake with coffee whilst having a chat – I knew almost everybody there! It *was* just like Community Lunch!

Then Annemieke started proceedings by praying. As she spoke, I felt the energy inside of me surge. It was as if she were talking to whatever was inside of me, and it was responding to her. Then Michele, another staff member, did the same, and my 'friend' surged again.

Prayers were followed by several contemporary Christian songs played on *YouTube*. They showed the lyrics on screen, and everybody joined in, regardless of singing ability. It made quite the racket, but it was a joyous racket.

I really liked some of the music, and had never expected Christian worship songs to be of the quality they were. As Kate later told me: "Some of my favourite worship music is the kind of song that your non-Christian friends would like, without realising it is Christian music."

The sing-along was followed by a Bible reading.

"You've brought your Bible, right?" Kate whispered into my ear.

"Err, no…" I responded, feeling foolish.

She opened her Bible app at the right passage (Acts 2), and passed it to me.

Thank God for Kate.

The lesson was about repenting for your sins. As various nationalities were present, everything was being done in English, with a variety of Bible versions being read out, and they confirmed everybody could understand and follow the lesson.

Jan and Annemieke then set up a role play, with Jan taking on the role of three very different types of people and their approach to repentance. They did it in such a way as to be hilarious and memorable. It was also very clear, as I could easily identify the three types of people Jan was portraying.

After this, we broke off into two groups, and sat in the garden discussing the three approaches, and how we related to the types of repentance Jan had shown so well.

We all got together for a final prayer, then more coffee and cakes. It was, for my first church service, a rather enjoyable, informative, and pleasant experience.

I knew I'd be back.

After church, we headed back to my house for my birthday celebration. A Spanish guy from the village was coming over to make a huge traditional Spanish paella for about thirty people. All the people from the church came down, except for those who were on duty at the *albergue*.

I was slightly worried because my friend Ed, who seemed to have made friends with everybody in the village, had taken it on himself to invite many villagers to my party. I knew what kind of party that would be, and I really didn't want them to arrive whilst the church group was at my house. In fact, I didn't really want a bunch of drunken, loud strangers to be at my house at all. He did it with my best interests at heart, as he wanted to introduce me to a lot of the locals. It was just that this changing version of me didn't really like the idea of that kind of party. However, it was done, and there was nothing I could do to avoid it now.

I had always hated celebrating my birthday, but this time I was really looking forward to it, with my new group of international friends.

It turned out to be just how I wanted it to be: kids, dogs, adults, good food, and good fun. Most people brought their swimming costumes, and we spent a lot of time playing in the pool.

At one point, Michele, along with a Dutch friend, laid their hands on Nath and prayed over her. Nath looked so relaxed and happy. It brought a tear to my eye. She later told me how relaxed she had felt during their praying. At the following Community Lunch, Nath felt sufficiently moved to give thanks for what they had done for her that day.

Despite my fears, no strangers arrived carrying six-packs. It was probably my best birthday party ever. And what made it even better was that Jan's two daughters were staying over in *Viana* that night, and they, along with Kate and I, were going to do a two-day walk along the *camino*, against the flow of traffic, back to their home in *Villamayor*, the following morning.

Monday 6 September 2021

It was to be my first real taste of hiking on the *Camino de Santiago*, as it entailed carrying backpacks and stopping the night in an *albergue* in the village of *Los Arcos*. To say I was looking forward to it would be an understatement. Obviously, it'd be a great time for Kate and I to spend some quality time together, but I was also excited about really getting to know Jan's two daughters: 17-year-old Rose, and her 15-year-old sister, Andie.

I set out from home at first light, marvelling at the deep red clouds on the horizon, and headed over to the house where the three ladies were staying. They soon joined me, and we picked up the *camino* and began walking along it against the flow of walkers. We knew that we'd meet many people walking the correct way, and that some would surely tell us we were going the wrong way.

As we headed out from *Viana* in the dawning light, we had a bet on how many times we would be told this. We each chose a number, and then we kept count of the amount of times we heard it.

As it was early, few pilgrims had yet to reach the approaches to *Viana*. We passed one or two and just wished them the traditional *buen camino* greeting, which they wished us in return.

Five kilometres out, and we reached *Bar Casita Lucia*, my usual stop for a second breakfast when out on my bike. We duly rested and had coffee with toasted sandwiches, and chatted with a few pilgrims doing the same.

After breakfast, we walked on until we reached an abandoned hermitage where we videoed an episode of all of us eating some unusual Dutch treat for the first time, for Kate's *Instagram* account.

We then continued on our way and, shortly afterwards, stopped for photos at the *Stone Forest*, which is a spot containing some interesting 'sculptures' made with piles of local stone, probably by the local guy that sits there with a table of drinks and snacks for pilgrims.

By now, the pilgrims were coming down the trail in greater numbers, and we were greeting and interacting with all of them in a fun-filled way. Quite a few informed us we were heading in the wrong direction, and we decided each time we were told that, we had to respond in a funny and unique way.

As we crested the next hill, we came face to face with a line of four pilgrims at a narrow part of the track. A middle-aged lady was leading the group as they bumped into us.

"Oh, you're going the wrong way…!" she said helpfully.

With the most serious face I could muster, I pointed back along the trail behind her and replied: "No, sorry. You're going the wrong way, not us!"

The lady immediately turned around and indicated for those behind her to turn around as well, which they all did.

Through laughter, we told them we were joking and – fortunately – they saw the funny side to it. We stopped and chatted with them for a while before continuing.

I was soon eliminated from the betting game, as I had chosen the rather low number of twelve for the amount of times we'd be told our direction was incorrect.

Another six kilometres later, we reached our first village of *Torres Del Río*. By now we were buzzing with joy, and one girl put some music on, so we began dancing together along the *camino*.

We entered our village for the night (*Los Arcos*) and checked into our *albergue*. I was aching all over, but I felt so happy. I only realised how much I ached once I lay back on my bed. My body was yearning for me to just stay there for the night, but we were starving, so we headed out.

We played card games for a few hours in the plaza before having dinner in a local café. We then made another eating video prior to returning to our accommodation, where we slept like babies.

Tuesday 7 September 2021

Early the next morning, we set off on our final, short leg to the girls' home town. Once again, we danced our way along the route, meeting every pilgrim walking the correct way towards us. We interacted with all of them, had some great laughs, and even had photos taken with some. A few even dared to suggest we were 'camino angels'.

We arrived in the village shortly after midday and met up with the group from Oasis Trails.

They took Kate and me to the guesthouse that the organisation had there, where we were to stay for the night, and where many of the staff and volunteers lived.

Kate had two roles during her visit to Europe: one being a missionary, and the other a journalist. Part of her job was to record interviews and write up stories during her travels. Part of this trip involved recording an interview with the couple who run Oasis Trails in Spain, so Kate and I went to the monastery and met up with Jan and Annemieke there.

Kate videoed an interview of the pair regarding their vision for the monastery. After that was done, we headed over to the organisation's *albergue* in *Villamayor* for my first ever pilgrim dinner. The meal was on the terrace at the front, and we sat amongst the dozen pilgrims who were staying there that night. It was a glorious evening, and we ate delicious food and chatted to people from all over the world. As the dinner came to a close, we watched the sun setting on the rooftops of the typical Spanish village. I have always loved the stunning view from that terrace.

Another first for me was an event that was to follow dinner. The *albergue* ran a 'Jesus Meditation' session, and Kate suggested we both attend. They invited all the pilgrims to come and relax, and to reflect on their journey so far, regardless of their beliefs.

I looked at the sign on the wall at the front of the *albergue*, advertising the session. It was the same as the one in the Oasis café[9] in *Viana*, which had caused me a little consternation a few months earlier. Far from being concerned now, I was actually quite looking forward to it, despite not knowing what really to expect. I hadn't meditated once in my life, and I certainly hadn't met Jesus.

We entered a converted stone barn at the side of the *albergue*, taking seats on the cushions and mats strewn on the floor. It was very cosy and comfortable, and, with about eight people, the atmosphere was very relaxing.

After sitting in silence for a short while, some contemporary Christian music was quietly played, as a softly spoken male voice gently told us to focus on nothing but the moment. We were advised to reflect on our individual journeys so far, and pose any questions we had into our minds.

My breathing became slower and deeper, and I forgot where I was.

A verse from the Bible was subsequently quietly read out before more music came on.

I'd never meditated before, so I just tried to focus and enjoy the feeling. I also thought I might ask some questions and somehow get some answers, though I didn't know how that might happen.

I relaxed myself as much as I could, and turned my focus towards my present situation. I didn't know what to say or do, so I asked a God that I didn't believe existed, to prove to me He did indeed actually exist.

I posed the same question to Him, over and over in my head, in the vain hope He might hear little, insignificant me, sitting on a converted barn floor, in a tiny village, somewhere in Spain. I mean, I wasn't even speaking aloud, so how could he hear what I was saying inside of my head?

It seemed slightly farcical to me. After all, I believed I was talking to nobody. And if I was wrong, and God did actually exist, who was I to be challenging the 'creator of the universe' to answer *me*? And why would He even bother with somebody like me?

As expected, all I got back from God was total silence.

I was about to give up trying, but then I heard a voice inside of my head – not God's, but Kate's: *God would love to hear from you.*

So I tried again, more earnestly this time.

Please, at least give me a sign. Just let me know, somehow, that I am wrong, and Kate is right, and that You exist.

Kate was always right, but *this* truth – this was just too astronomically absurd for me to accept as real.

Whilst I was sitting in silence, inviting or praying for God to have a little chat with me, the lyrics of a song[10], which was playing quietly in the background, came into my thoughts. It went something like this:

"Lord that is loved... You set me free..."

The phrase kept repeating itself to me.

"You set me free... You set me free..."

Why was I noticing these particular words? Did this phrase mean

COME TO THE TABLE

something to me? And then I thought of the little bird trapped in the monastery, about to kill itself as it slammed repeatedly into the windows. Until I *set it free*.

And the other baby bird a week later, entangled in the guy's hair, about to be swatted by enormous hands. Until I *set him free* too.

Were these little birds somehow the signs that I had been so desperate to see? Or were they just weird coincidences?

Kate: *"There are no coincidences."*

And then I remembered another bird in this story: the owl that had 'miraculously' appeared when I'd first met Kate, just as we had spoken of the word *owl* on the day my depression lifted. And then the eagle the day Ed arrived?

As these thoughts ran through my mind, the emotion inside of me spoke – in fact, it surged. It took my breath away, and tears formed in my eyes. I wiped my cheeks and opened my eyes, looking guardedly around the room at the other people present.

Nobody had noticed.

I thought these incidents had all been bizarre coincidences, which was a concept Kate just didn't believe in. In fact, all of my new friends felt the same. Kate claimed they were just God's way of getting our attention. It made sense – they certainly got my attention.

Encounters with complete strangers that led to other events happening, such as when my path crossed with Wes and Sherry at the beginning of this story, were referred to as DAs (Divine Appointments). Throughout this story, I had suspected such events had somehow been pre-planned.

These DAs and coincidences were mounting up, stacking up against me. Such an excessive amount, in such a short period. As a writer, I knew that if I wrote a story with such unbelievable and continual coincidences in it, I'd lose the reader, as the story would just be too far-fetched to be acceptable.

And yet, there they were – really happening to me. I just didn't know *why* they were happening. Nothing this intense had happened to me before, so why now?

I thought over the ramifications of my dilemma. It was a massive decision to make; if Kate was wrong, and they *were* mere coincidences, then it was all for nothing. But if I accepted they were just too unbelievable to be coincidences, and that something else was at play here, then Kate had the only alternative explanation for me. And if Kate was right, then my entire belief system of the last fifty-five years had been completely wrong.

It meant either absolutely nothing or *absolutely everything*.

And then, over and above these incidents, there was that 'emotion' inside of me, now on full throttle, which had entered me in that church seven weeks ago, and had been doing all kinds of unexpected and wonderful things to me since. As it was doing to me then – the thing that Kate said was the Holy Spirit.

It was just too fantastical to accept, too impossible to deal with, and I felt trapped in a corner, with only one path available to me, and I didn't enjoy being trapped.

It was a 'fight or flight' moment for me, and I was still fighting it with what little strength I had left in me.

Before long, the meditation session was over and we had a general feedback chat amongst the group before we all left the barn.

Kate and I got a ride back to the guesthouse. We walked up the two flights of stairs together in relative silence, as I was deep in thought, the emotion still surging in my chest.

Those birds? Surely that can't be a message from God..? I thought, as I turned my bedroom door handle, pushing the door open.

On the bedroom wall, directly across from the door, was a painting. Sat on top of the picture frame was a wild bird. It looked directly at me and then flew out of the open window.

Wednesday 8 September 2021

I'd briefly met an American pilgrim called Clive[11] at the guesthouse yesterday. He'd suffered a foot injury on the *camino* and was having trouble walking, so he'd stopped to rest up for a while. Jan had invited him to stay at the guesthouse for as long as he needed. He intended to get the injury checked over by a doctor if there was no improvement over the next day or two, and then continue on his pilgrimage.

At 7.00am I woke up, instantly wide awake, and immediately thought of Clive's injury. I opened Google, checked something out, and within minutes I knew what was wrong with him. I went down to the kitchen and found him there, quietly having a coffee, with his injured foot resting on a stool.

I asked him if I could examine his foot and discussed his symptoms with him.

"You have a stress fracture," I told him confidently. I also had to tell him that his pilgrimage was over, as he needed to stay off the foot until it healed, and therefore wouldn't be able to walk on it for a good number of weeks. I also reminded him I wasn't a doctor, and he would need to get it x-rayed to confirm the fracture.

(Later that day, he saw a doctor who confirmed my diagnosis. His pilgrimage was over after just a week of walking, but he accepted what had happened, as he believed God had brought him to the community for a reason. A week later, he flew back to the States[12].)

I grabbed a coffee and sat chatting with Clive about his life, and told him of my story so far. Early risers began coming in for coffee, and, by 11.00am, the entire community had gathered there for coffee and cake. They had come to the guesthouse to attend what they called 'Carpet Time'. I'd heard people speak of it many times, so, today – again, under Kate's instruction and guidance – I was to sit in on it for the very first time.

Carpet Time is basically the community's daily morning worship, which is done in the lounge of the guesthouse. The lounge is full of carpets and rugs (hence the name), a beanbag, musical instruments, and complete wall paintings depicting biblical stories, etc.

After coffee and cake in the kitchen, everybody finds a comfortable seat in the lounge, and one of the staff members leads the service: prayer, music videos, readings, and a lesson. Anybody can join in at any time, or ask questions, or sit and do nothing. Afterwards, there is more coffee, cake, and conversation.

It was a really pleasant experience, one that I found to be very relaxing and inviting.

After this, we all went over to the monastery for Community Lunch. Whilst there, I told Jan of the bird I'd discovered in my bedroom the night before, and he stated that they'd *never* had birds inside of the guesthouse, although they get them inside of the monastery.

Sherry, who was listening, laughed. "God certainly knows how to get *your* attention, Dave!"

Sunday 12 September 2021

I attended my second church. I was actually really enjoying going. Along with the Carpet Time session, I was learning so much, especially in relation to the contents of the Bible, and how events actually match up across the entire book so much so that, again, you could not have called them coincidences.

Coincidence finally felt like a poor choice of word for events happening around me. I needed another way to refer to them, so I began referring to any further coincidences as *the C-word*.

"Oh, that's weird. Yet another C-word just happened."

We'd been planning the upcoming trip all week, so, after church, Kate and I, along with another volunteer, were going to drive to the other side of the French border, park the car up, and walk for two days along the *camino*, from the main starting point.

We'd heard from many pilgrims how difficult this initial stage was, as it involved going up and over the mountain range that separates France from Spain: the *Pyrenees*. For this reason, we wanted to experience it for ourselves.

As we drove away from the monastery, we travelled up the *camino* to visit two famous landmarks on it: the *Puente la Reina* (an 11th-century pilgrim foot-bridge in the town with the same name) and *Alto de Perdón* (Hill of Forgiveness).

From there, we headed past *Pamplona* and across the French border to a beautiful small town, officially recognised as the start of the *Camino de Santiago: Saint-Jean-Pied-de-Port*.

Whilst out dining in the delightful town that evening, I received a message from my ex telling me she was in France. I told her I was also in France. Sadly, that message created a barrage of messages that was to cause me unnecessary stress over what was truly a magical two days.

Unbeknown to me, that simple communication was to set in motion a chain of events that ultimately helped lead to the conclusion of this story.

After dinner, we spent the night at an *albergue* in the town.

Monday 13 September 2021

Just before dawn, Kate and I headed out on *The Camino Francés*[13]. As we navigated our way out of the sleeping town in the dark, we began ascending a slight gradient out of the town. We had left the *albergue* with two other pilgrims, but, as we wound our way along the tarmac track and up an ever-steepening gradient, we came across an increasing number of other early starters.

Our route was only twenty-four kilometres in total split over the two days, with a planned overnight stop at an *albergue* situated almost at the top of the mountain, with spectacular views. The distance to our *albergue* was just eight kilometres, but the ascent was becoming very steep.

As we climbed, I received six angry messages from my ex following my message about my being in France. This was seriously distracting me and spoiling my experience, so I muted her for the day.

Kate and I stopped often to take photographs because the higher we went the greater the scenery became. We also witnessed the sun rising over the *Pyrenees*. With every passing minute, the sky continuously changed colour, and Kate had to stop constantly to photograph the views, or to just sit and take it all in.

During this time, we met and chatted to many pilgrims, as the town below us quickly came alive to the buzz of dozens of excited pilgrims, setting off on the first stage of their *camino*. Some were quite elderly or unfit, and many were struggling to make the ascent, whilst others were racing past us intending to do what we were doing over two days, in just one day! For that, you needed to be very fit and prepared.

Many of the struggling pilgrims would reach us, and, as we engaged them in conversation, they'd wisely choose to stop for a breather.

We chatted with everybody who passed and gave the strugglers and stragglers some motivation and encouragement as needed. They would then continue on up the hill. Shortly afterwards, we'd catch them up, chat to them some more, then overtake them before stopping for more pics. In this way, we were constantly leap-frogging each other, and we'd do a quick welfare check on them as we did so. We'd become friendly with many pilgrims by the time we reached our overnight destination.

By eleven o'clock we had arrived at our *albergue* at *Orisson*, and, after checking in, had a well-deserved beer, whilst we enjoyed the most spectacular views across the mountain range from the terrace. We met many of the people we'd spoken to on the ascent, and some stopped at the *albergue* for the night, whilst others continued up the mountain and down the other side.

The community dinner at the *albergue* that night was a very special event for both Kate and I. Approximately twenty-five pilgrims of various ages and nationalities were sitting down to eat together. After dinner, each person was required to stand and introduce themselves, say where they came from, and why they were doing the *camino*. Naturally, there was quite a mix of reasons, but, every now and again, a fully-grown adult would be in tears as they explained to a group of complete strangers, a very personal and moving reason for doing the pilgrimage. Hearts were opened and souls bared in the most moving manner possible. It was a beautiful way to start the *camino*, and, once again, friendships were instantly formed.

We made many friendships on that short hike up the mountain. I was later able to meet many of these people as they walked for another week or more, when they finally arrived in my home village of *Viana* on the *camino*.

Tuesday 14 September 2021

The following day, we again set off before sunrise and continued on up the mountains on a much longer and higher leg of the journey, until we arrived at the summit. I turned my phone off all day to conserve the battery. It was the most remote, and therefore riskiest, part of the trip, so I really needed the phone battery to last until we reached our destination. I also wanted to prevent any more unpleasant messages from ruining the day.

Each summit that we reached (and assumed to be the top) revealed yet another summit further on. It took a long time before we were suddenly heading down the other side of the *Pyrenees*, and into the Spanish town of *Roncesvalles*. It was here where most pilgrims then stopped for the night.

We had a late lunch there at a bar, and bumped into a guy we'd met on the mountains, who had done the two-day hike in a single day, and who was then too tired to continue in the morning, having chosen to stay an extra day in the village to recover.

After dinner, I caught the bus back to *Saint-Jean-Pied-de-Port* to collect the car, before returning to *Roncesvalles* to collect Kate and the other girl with us. We then headed home.

The experience of walking for just two days was magical and gave Kate and me a real taste of the *camino*. We both just wanted to keep on walking – if we had, we'd have made it home in one week.

There is something really special that transcends mere walking on the *Camino de Santiago*. It is hard work, yet relaxing. You are amongst strangers and yet make friends for life. You come from all backgrounds, and classes, and abilities, yet it is a leveller – it makes you all equal.

As Laura, a passing pilgrim, succinctly put it: "Everything is hurting, but it's great!"

People walk the *camino* for all kinds of reasons: for something to do, something to tick off a list, for fitness or health reasons, a challenge, to seek answers, to find themselves, or simply to escape life for a few weeks.

Whatever the reason, the *camino* gives everybody time and space to think. For me, it was a pleasure to be away from all the C-words and other weird stuff that had been happening in my life over the previous few months.

And it gave *me* plenty of time to think.

Wednesday 15 September 2021

Having returned home from our taster of the *camino*, we went to the Community Lunch and shared lots of tales of our adventures. It was whilst here that I started getting a lot more of those stressful messages from my ex. Incredibly, she was threatening to report me to the police for theft of her company car, which she'd left with me to use, as she didn't drive. Clearly, this was a civil issue, and certainly not a police matter, and yet she eventually advised me she had reported the car as stolen.

I was bombarded with fourteen angry messages on this day – from midday until 11.00pm. Again, for my sanity, I had to mute the chat.

After my previous arrest and incarceration in a primitive jail, this threat had to be taken seriously. It was something that I just did not need or want in my life anymore. I couldn't believe that she'd forgotten the hell she'd put me through before. It weighed me down so much – from being so happy and full of joy for quite a while now, to where a sudden depression hit me hard again.

I went home that afternoon, not knowing what to do.

I attended the Alpha course in the evening, and learned that Jesus had died on the cross for our sins, and I had nothing to say about it. I didn't speak all evening, such was my stress.

That night, when I got home, I set myself up for another C-word, as well as clearly showing my changing beliefs. I had to write something to escape from my thoughts, so I opened up my book, *Listen to the Camino*, and rewrote the introduction to it:

> *"The Inspiration for this book:*
> *One day, whilst out exploring the camino, I had a weird surge of emotions whilst walking around a beautiful church at the back of a*

disused monastery. As a non-believer, this disturbed me greatly. Investigating further, I discovered the remnants of a Saint called Veremundo located in the church. Enquiries later revealed that Veremundo was in fact the Patron Saint of Pilgrims travelling through the ancient Kingdom of Navarra, and that most pilgrims were not only unaware of this, but that they simply walked past his beautiful monastery, without ever once stepping inside to acknowledge his legacy to pilgrims walking the route today. They will happily drink from the free wine fountain nearby – one that only exists because of his actions all those years ago.

I feel that the modern world is too busy to remember the stories of the past, yet most of us routinely take advantage of the present, such as free wine, without even thinking of why it is there at all. Many pilgrims simply see the camino as something they have to 'complete', just to tick it off their list of achievements. Yet that is not what the camino is about. Saint Veremundo worked tirelessly with the pilgrims passing by his monastery over a thousand years ago, even getting into trouble for helping them too much! He is an integral part of the history of the ancient Kingdom of Navarra – the first province you walk across on entering Spain – and he will be the Patron Saint of you as you walk your pilgrimage across Navarra, through his home town, as you drink his wine and pass his monastery. He is on the camino with you, looking out for you, and ensuring you reach the next province (La Rioja) safely.

I believe Veremundo gave me a message when I first discovered him, almost forgotten about at the back of that beautiful church. I'll never forget the emotions that hit me that day immediately after viewing his relics. He knew I was a writer, that I loved the camino and the people on it, and that I was on my way to visit, for the first time, another abandoned monastery nearby, which had recently been purchased by a Christian organisation called Oasis Trails. This organisation hopes to renovate this beautiful building and make it into a community for people on a journey of faith and a place for pilgrims. I was bowled over by their vision, and a few days later, the idea for this book was born. I surprised myself when I announced, without thinking about it, that I would donate all the profits from it to this organisation, to help them realise that beautiful, ambitious dream.

There is no doubt that a chain of unusual and coincidental events led to this book being written, many of which I couldn't even explain back then. As a lifelong atheist, the day that Veremundo spoke to me was the day I realised that my life was about to change.

Veremundo instructed me to write this book for pilgrims, so that they have the opportunity to connect with the ancient history of the path they are walking, and can discover incredible stories along the entire length of the camino. This book also contains stories of people from the present, as history is still being made along this wondrous path, as well as lots of useful tips and help for you, all written to make your pilgrimage as rewarding as possible, whatever the reason you are doing it. I want to help you, just as Veremundo would have wanted to, and just as he wants me to do."

Clearly, this updated passage shows that my beliefs were all over the place at this point. My not believing in God, yet being willing to accept that a dead saint had somehow spoken to me from beyond the grave, shows how confused I was back then. I was still unwilling to believe that God could exist, but had taken a step towards believing in something that was far from atheism. However, I felt I was being *called* somehow to write this book, even if I was still unwilling to see that it was God who was doing the calling.

I've since learned that saints don't call people, and they don't walk with you on the *camino*. Only God can do this. Saint Veremundo was clearly an amazing man who had a big heart for God's people, and he wanted to help them on their journey so much that he often got into trouble for doing so. But his work is done, and we should leave him to rest in heaven.

Thursday 16 September 2021

Today was to be a momentous day in my journey. There was a reckoning about to happen, which I would have to accept and move forward, or refuse to accept and change my path.

I woke up depressed, and so needed to talk to somebody. Kate was out on the *camino* with the Canadians, giving out free water, and, as she had no data plan, she was completely unreachable.

After busying myself with some essential household chores, I headed out on the *camino* on my bike. I met pilgrims, had breakfast at *Bar Casita Lucia*, and raced down a long, steep hill, crazily fast. The exhilaration was just what I needed. Whenever I did this hill ride, Kate would tell me to be careful and to get my 'eternity sorted out first'.

I met Ed for lunch in the village, and, over a beer, we discussed my current situation.

It was almost as if I was being given a glimpse of my past life, and reminded of how unhappy it had been, and that this newfound joy was something not to be taken lightly. Was I being warned that I needed to move forward if I wished to continue to feel the elation I now felt in my new life?

I hated this feeling of sadness that had engulfed me out of nowhere, which had taken away my joy, my spirit.

By evening time, I had to speak to Kate about it, as I was still no better. She was working at the café, and suggested I come over. I told her I would, but that it wasn't something we could speak about in front of the others.

On arrival, we made a group video for Kate's *Instagram* series, called *Katey Eats Stuff*. They are always fun to be involved in, and this certainly helped me to forget the situation for a while.

Whilst preparing for this, the others asked me questions regarding the car situation, as they'd detected that something was amiss. I wasn't ready to talk openly about this, so Kate quickly stepped in, changing the subject for me.

Once the video was complete, Kate finished work and offered to walk with me so that we could chat. We went to the ruins of *San Pedro Church* at the end of the street. Behind it was a garden with spectacular views across the *Ebro Valley*, and, as usual, it was quiet and deserted. It always upset me that most pilgrims walked past this church without seeing the amazing structure and the breathtaking views hidden behind it.

We leaned against the top of the old fortress wall and looked out across the landscape, watching the sun as it began to set with a promise of a beautiful display across the valley.

We started chatting about last night's Alpha course, and I admitted I hadn't really followed it much, and therefore didn't understand how Jesus dying on the cross meant *my* sins were forgiven. She explained it to me in a few simple sentences, and I instantly understood.

I then explained to her what had been happening regarding the car since we'd arrived in France. I was already feeling much better after making the video, and felt silly for asking to talk to her about it now.

Kate was shocked by what was happening, as she knew about my previous experience in a cell, and was horrified by it. She told me she didn't feel it would come to me being arrested again.

Kate believed that as people get closer to God the enemy gets upset and does all he can to disrupt it from happening. Kate knew I was moving towards believing and expected there to be action against me to prevent it.

"I feel God is calling you, Dave," she said. "He wants *you*. Why *won't* you hear Him?"

It was a fair question, but I just couldn't come up with an answer that made any sense.

We then chatted about Nath, and how she had thanked the two ladies who had prayed over her on my birthday.

"I mean, look how far you two have come!" said Kate. "If that had happened a few months ago, I think she might have freaked out!"

I laughed. Spot on, as always.

After a brief silence, Kate spoke again, quietly and thoughtfully.

"Seriously, Dave? What *more* does He have to do to get your attention?" she asked.

I clearly frustrated Kate with my inability to see what was happening to me, around me, and in me.

I wasn't used to Kate speaking quietly to me like this. I was used to her shouting at me in frustration, being snarky, stamping her feet even – all in good humour, and in the way I needed someone to speak to me.

But this was a completely different approach. This was a distressed, hurting, and unhappy Kate. This was a Kate I hadn't really seen before, and I was clearly the one causing her the hurt by my lack of action.

"I love you, and I love Nath, and I want you *both* to be in eternity with me."

This she said with tears falling down her cheeks. The pain I was obviously causing her cut me to the heart. Whatever the reality of all of this, Kate truly believed what she was saying, and my lack of acceptance of it was causing her so much distress. She pleaded with me, still tearful.

"Why won't you *believe* me?"

There wasn't really another question she could have asked me at that point. It was perhaps the last question to ask, the end of the road, and I still didn't have an answer for her.

Kate had never let me down before. Kate was *always* right, and now, by my inaction, I implied that she was wrong about this, and yet I had no proof to say that she was wrong. Quite the contrary, over the previous months, I'd witnessed so much that I simply couldn't explain using *my* beliefs, yet *her* explanations made perfect sense to me. I just couldn't, for some stubborn reason, accept them.

I fumbled for something to say. "I feel things, Kate, I really do. I've never felt so happy, so at peace, and overjoyed. It is hard to explain the difference in me now… You've brought so much to me, I could never thank you enough for what you've done for me."

"Just think what you could do for the people *you* love! Think of how you could give this to Nath! If you just accepted Jesus into your heart, think of how you could change the lives of others."

I let those words sink in. This wasn't about me, wasn't about people-collecting, chalking up converts, and increasing the tally. This was about sharing something so beautiful that it was almost impossible for a mere man like me to put into words. The joy I had been feeling of late was not because of Kate, but of where Kate had led me – one way or the other, she had brought me closer to Jesus. And the closer I got, the stronger my feelings of joy were. And yet I was still incapable of total acceptance.

Knowing that I could give such joy to the people I love – *to Nath* – was a beautiful realisation. What a gift to give to others!

As we chatted, I heard some faint music coming from somewhere in the deserted gardens.

"Where's that coming from?" I asked, deflecting the conversation slightly.

Kate took me to a hole in the lawn near to the church, where a small speaker was hidden, playing some elevator music. I'd never noticed any music there before. We walked back to the wall and continued chatting about my situation.

Kate's frustration at my refusal to acknowledge God was finally coming to the fore. I was being a really stubborn fool, and I don't know how she put up with me back then. What more could be done to show me the truth? Was there *anything* that would convince me?

With tears in her eyes, she continued. "I think God is calling you, Dave, as He has a job for you to do." She paused for thought. "I think He is calling you for your writing."

There's the C-word again. I smiled, shaking my head. *There just had to be one, didn't there?*

I felt the pull too. A calling. And it made perfect sense to me. I was now writing a book for pilgrims to help them on their *camino*, the profits were going to a project to restore an old monastery for people seeking answers, I was writing *Come to the Table* about my potential path towards Jesus, and I felt that both books were going to sell well.

"Yes!" she responded to my reaction. "And you've already sold your books to hundreds of eager pilgrims, so you'd better get on and write them! Just think of the impact that such a story as yours could have on people around the world. If you can bring such joy to just *one* person – to Nath – imagine what that'd feel like if you could do it for thousands of people?"

I told her about the rewrite I'd done, where I'd written in my book

that I believed Saint Veremundo had *'instructed me to write this book'*
and that *'he gave me a message…'*

I just could not call this a coincidence. I'd done the rewrite – reflecting
a close similarity with Kate's current message – just last night, when I was
feeling down and not really in my usual mood for writing. I just felt I had
to write it, and now she was telling me what I basically said in my re-write
twelve hours earlier.

I said a saint had called me, but she'd corrected me: it was God who
does the calling, not the saints. The result was the same – we had
simultaneously agreed that I was being called for my writing.

As I was telling her this, I heard the quiet elevator music playing in the
garden change to a song that had become to mean so much to me lately.

I paused mid-sentence and smiled.

"Is that *Amazing Grace*[14] that's playing?"

Kate smiled back at me, nodding knowingly. "Uh-huh."

Had she been expecting that to happen?

It was a C-word on top of another C-word. I was no longer surprised
– I was getting to the point of expecting such bizarre events to happen to
me every day.

As I stared at her smiling, almost victorious face, the sun quickly
turned a gloriously golden colour, illuminating the stone of the church
behind us. It glowed like it was made of gold, and I just had to take a
picture, capturing that moment – and our shadows – forever.

This was undoubtedly a pivotal moment in my journey. Without this
event, I don't think the rest of the story would have unfolded as it did. It
was a combination of the cutting realisation that I was breaking Kate's
heart with my intransigence about what was clearly, and constantly, there
for me to see – an understanding of the fact that I could pass this amazing
gift on to other people I love, and the C-words that seem to support
events that were happening to me. I was now accepting that these
C-words were, in fact, messages to me, and they could only be messages
from one place: from God.

Everything that had happened so far had led me to this decisive
moment in the churchyard. In hindsight, the issue with the car and the

The ruins of San Pablo Church, Viana,
with the shadows of Kate and I just visible bottom right

threat of being sent to jail was an essential chapter in my story – had it not happened, that moment in the church would not have come to pass.

It was the message of love that day that finally got through to me. The love Kate had for me and Nath, the love she has for Jesus, and the love Jesus has for me. The whole story is one of total, supreme love. That love showered on me touched my heart in a way I cannot put into words.

We all desire to be loved for who we are, and when we are loved without question, we are completed.

God had turned the enemy's actions to His own advantage.

> *Kate: "Dave seems to be changing every day. He's not just happier and more enjoyable to be around, but now, when something is going on, he wants to talk about it and he wants answers. His disputes against God and claims of unbelief are weaker and weaker. He seems to be understanding and accepting, but just not admitting. He asks me questions, but instead of fighting the answers or trying to make it about something other than God, he just weakly responds that he doesn't get it.*

It is so frustrating for me because I feel like his heart gets it, but his logical brain still has control over his mouth. He seems to accept what I say, and just the fact that he comes to me with these questions shows me he's believing that what I'm telling him is the truth, but he just doesn't want to give in and admit he's been wrong all this time. I can feel that he is so close.

Tonight, I was crying in frustration as we talked. It breaks my heart that he just can't seem to accept that it doesn't matter what he was wrong about, Jesus wants to have a relationship with him. It's almost like he is scared to admit that someone could love him that much. If he could just take the last step of becoming truly vulnerable and submitted to Jesus, there would be nothing left between them."

PAGE 111

[8] "The Case for Christ" by Lee Strobel. ISBN-13: 9780310226055

PAGE 117

[9] The Oasis café had originally been run by Oasis Trails, hence the similarity in name and function.

PAGE 118

[10] Despite numerous efforts, we've never been able to identify this song.

PAGE 120

[11] Not his real name.

PAGE 121

[12] We are still in touch, and he hopes to return to complete his *camino* one day.

PAGE 123

[13] The Camino Francés, translated as The French Route, is the most well-trodden and most famous of the twelve routes that pilgrims can take to reach Santiago.

PAGE 133

[14] "Amazing Grace", my late father's favourite song of all time, despite his being a non-believer. I had played it almost daily since my mum told me which version he loved, and now an instrumental version was playing out of a hole in the ground, in that almost empty churchyard, as we simultaneously agreed that my writing was most likely a calling of God.

CHAPTER 12

TOP OF THE MOUNTAIN

Saturday 18 September 2021

In the morning, Kate, Nath, and I walked up to *Casita Lucía* on the *camino*, the small wooden bar for pilgrims, just before *Viana*.

Bar Casita Lucia, on the Camino de Santiago, Viana, Navarra

I'd asked Nath along, as I really hoped that she'd feel the pull of the *camino*.

Just before we reached the café, we bumped into a large group of about a dozen pilgrims who had paused for a rest. We stopped and chatted with them. As usual, they asked us why we were walking the wrong way, and where we were from. When they discovered Nath was Brazilian, a French guy in the group started singing and dancing with her. Nath danced right back at him in the middle of the *camino*, in the centre of a group of strangers. It was a truly magical moment.

My plan worked. Later, Nath told me she intended to do the *camino* the following summer!

That night, whilst in the café with Kate, we met a pilgrim who told us of an earlier incident on *Mount Perdón*, the place we had visited on our way to France. He'd met four American military veterans, who had been walking the *camino*, when one of them (named Ted) had collapsed with a suspected heart attack. He had been airlifted off by helicopter and admitted to Pamplona hospital.

The pilgrim mentioned the name of one of the other vets, which was a very unusual family name, and Kate suspected she might know the family. Our mutual friend sent some messages to them regarding this, and I was genuinely expecting the C-word here – I wouldn't have been surprised in the least. However, it wasn't the family Kate knew.

The three fellow walkers (Bob, Chris, and Chris) had continued their *camino*, as they were walking in memory of the fallen.

Sunday 19 September 2021

Kate and I went to church together very early. The founders of Oasis Trails were staying at the monastery for a while, and had kindly accepted Kate's offer of an interview in her role as a missions journalist. We drove directly there, introductions were made, and we sat and had coffee and a chat with them. We spoke of my story so far, and then Kate set up her camera and interviewed them.

The Canadians had taken the other volunteer at the café to experience a Spanish church in the nearby city of *Logroño*, so, after the interview,

Kate and I went to church with the founders.

Monday 20 September 2021

Following the dispute over my ex's car, I had decided never to drive that car again. It meant that I now had to use my own car. Nath had been using mine to drive herself to college, then to work afterwards, before driving it back home. So we agreed she could drive her aunt's car, in place of me, and I'd get my car back. There was only one problem – it was three times the size of my car, so Nath wanted me to give her some lessons in it until she was accustomed to driving it.

So, at lunchtime, I decide to go to *Casita Lucía* for a second breakfast as usual, but instead of cycling or walking there, we'd go by car so that Nath could drive, with me instructing.

We had our usual breakfast there, and then Nath drove us back to the village. As we entered the outskirts, I saw three pilgrims walking along the road, well off the *camino*. I thought they were probably lost, and I had an overwhelming urge to stop and check on them, but Nath was running late for work. So she drove on, planning on dropping me off at the top of the hill, so that I could walk into the village and home, and she would then drive on to work in the city.

As I was getting out of the car, she started getting messages from work. Her aunt was running late, so she didn't have to race off after all. As we sat and discussed our options, I saw the three lost pilgrims arrive at the top of the hill. They went over to the bus timetables and read them, so I walked over to them to see if they needed any help.

They said they were from the USA, and that they were three military veterans – but had started out as a foursome.

"Ah," I said. "You must be Bob, Chris, and Chris…"

The shock on their faces was clear.

"… and Ted was the one who had the medical problem on *Perdón*, and had to go back home?"

I told them of how I knew their story, whilst thinking of what the chances were of me bumping into them, well off the *camino*, whilst – unusually – driving the car that day. This 'coincidence' was later confirmed as a Divine Appointment, as it eventually led me to a person who had a profound impact on me and my story.

They stayed in the village for lunch and invited me to join them. They also corrected me in relation to Ted – he was still in the hospital in Pamplona, and didn't speak any Spanish.

My heart immediately went out to him, and, over lunch, I promised them I would visit Pamplona to see if I could help him in any way, so they passed me his details.

That evening, Nath, Ed, and I were invited to the home of the Canadians for a farewell party for Kate. It was a fun night of pizza and games.

Tuesday 21 September 2021

After speaking to five different members of staff on his ward, I finally got confirmation that I could come and visit Ted, and, in the meantime, they'd pass him my number for him to call me.

I drove the forty-five minute trip to the hospital and spent thirty minutes finding a parking space. When I finally arrived at the ward, I found Ted in his bed, talking to a nurse who spoke English. I waited nearby until they had finished.

Ted was slightly older than me, but he had this supreme calmness and genuineness about him. Every word he spoke seemed to be perfectly thought out, carefully measured, and beautifully delivered.

I finally introduced myself and explained the background to my visit. He was extremely grateful and, as we chatted, he told me a little about his life. He'd been a fighter pilot in the Vietnam War, flying off aircraft carriers. After the war, he had risen through the ranks in the navy, eventually becoming a naval commander of his own ship. He then became a priest and continued to serve as a naval chaplain.

He told me of his experience on *Mount Perdón*, and of his desire to fly home at the earliest opportunity. He didn't want to stay around for treatment, preferring to get it back home in the States. I promised to be available to him in any way he needed. I even invited him to stay at the guesthouse of Oasis Trails if he needed a few days to relax before he left, knowing that Jan would be absolutely fine with this.

I also told him of my story so far, before saying goodbye.

As I bade him farewell, he asked if he could pray over me. We were standing in the corridor with patients and visitors walking past. A few months ago, I'd have been flustered, embarrassed, and apologetic, and would have probably run off down the corridor. To have Father Ted pray over me felt like such an honour, so I stood in the corridor with my head bowed, as he put his hands on me and prayed aloud, in front of all of those people.

His prayer over me lasted a good few minutes, and the words he said that day went through me and on to some other place. I cannot remember a single word of what he said. All I do recall is that, as I walked out of that ward, I did so in tears.

I was incapable of driving, so I hunted down the hospital café and sat and drank coffee, still with tears running down my cheeks. People looked at me in sympathy.

Father Ted had had a heart attack whilst on holiday in a foreign country, far from home, where he didn't speak the language, with a mistrust of the health system, without his family or friends present, and *he* prayed for *me*.

Did he see my situation as being more dire than his?

It took me about an hour before I felt ready to drive home.

Wednesday 22 September 2021

Kate was at the airport again, on her way to Germany. As usual, she had time to talk to me.

> *Me, 9.40am: "…he prayed over me as I was about to leave and said the most beautiful prayer for me ever. I was in tears for about an hour… it moved me so much, I can't explain."*
>
> *Kate: "I guess I have a hard time understanding what can move you to tears, but not also to action. I'm not being snarky, I'm genuinely curious. Because my tears are tied to the filling of the Holy Spirit and the gratefulness I feel, but that all comes with the*

salvation I've accepted and the giving of myself to Him."

Me: "He's one of those people you meet who speaks slowly, and every word is perfectly thought out and delivered, and totally convincing."

Kate: "That's not an answer. That's an evasion."

Me: "I'm still trying to fathom out what is happening to me. I feel the Spirit – strongly too – and I feel a huge compulsion to help people all the time. It seems to get stronger each day. Perhaps I'm unsure of what comes next, or what to do next?"

I'd just taken another enormous step. I had just confirmed that it was the Holy Spirit that I felt within me. I also hinted that I was now ready to move further forward, whilst not being really sure of what I had to do to do so. I was basically reaching out to Kate for the next step, knowing that she'd be there for me, even whilst negotiating her way through a busy airport.

Kate: "Do you want to talk about what comes next? What comes next is accepting the gift of salvation, asking Jesus to have your heart and your life, and dying to self and living for Him (meaning it's no longer about you and your glory or fame or whatever, but about Him and His glory and His Kingdom)… complete surrender to Him."

Me: "That feels like a HUGE leap. How do I do that, and would anything change? I must sound like a complete buffoon, but please remember, a few months ago I would have laughed at this kind of talk."

I was obviously still hesitating here and worried that too much might change too soon. I was also clearly in very unfamiliar territory.

Kate: "You don't sound like a buffoon at all. And it is a huge leap, but compared to being tortured and crucified on a cross, it's really not so big." 😊

Her response made me laugh, and I felt slightly ridiculous about my fears.

Kate explained how my life would change – people I know might laugh at me, or criticise me, or even hate me.

> Kate: *"But, amazingly, it's also easy because you don't have to carry it. And the joy that comes with it is far beyond anything else."*

I voiced my fears of what I might have to give up – my dreams and ambitions – and Kate told me of all the things she had given up to follow her path.

> Kate: *"There's an amazing peace when you give up on yourself and what you want, and give it all to Him."*

Unbeknown to me, immediately after we finished chatting, Kate contacted Annemieke at the monastery and updated her.

> Kate: *"… I'm at the airport, waiting for my flight. I wanted to share with you that Dave has been asking a lot of really good questions about salvation this morning. I'm encouraging him to talk with Jan, or you, or Michele at lunch today, but I think he is nervous. Would one of you try to have an intentional conversation with him? I'm not sure if he's ready, but I think he needs to have answers from more than just me, and he really respects you. I know you will discern where his heart really is, and not judge him for his doubts, but encourage him."*
>
> Observation by Kate:
> *"I hated not being there for you, but I trusted Jan, Annemieke, and Michele, and I knew they would be there for you, and be very supportive, and I prayed for you. Annemieke immediately responded with joy and enthusiasm."*

I went to Community Lunch early, as I was expecting to have to go to Pamplona to help Father Ted check out of the hospital. Whilst waiting for his call, I worked at the monastery with the founder, digging up the old floor with a pneumatic drill.

Father Ted later sent me a message saying he didn't need my help after all, and he was now on his way back to the States. He addressed me as Brother David.

After lunch, I sat with the founder and his wife over coffee, and spoke to them more about my story, and where I was at on my path. They agreed with each other that I 'believed already'. My heart was there, but my mouth wouldn't admit to it. I had even started wearing a rubber bracelet given to me earlier, stating that 'God is real'.

After lunch, Annemieke wrote to Kate:

> *"He talked to Jan, and wants to talk with the one, two, or three of us soon. Hopefully tomorrow."* 🙏

In the evening, I went to the home of Wes and Sherry for dinner, followed by the Alpha course. During some technical difficulties with the video, Ed and I chatted about my position. Ed said that he felt sure that I was close to being baptised and jokingly told the others to go and get the bath filled. He asked me what was actually keeping me from giving myself to Jesus, as he felt it was close to happening.

"I don't know," I replied. I thought hard about it and then began speaking.

I felt like I had been on a long and steep climb up a mountain over the past few months. A few months earlier, every element of my life had somehow been re-arranged, and had conspired together to push, prod, and nudge me ever forwards, towards that summit.

It was like the chess game of my life – in which I knew exactly where every piece was – had suddenly been rearranged by some invisible, external force. The once familiar game board was now unrecognisable to me. It was my turn, and yet I couldn't see how to play, how to make my move, as it was all so different to me.

I now stood just before the summit of that mountain I'd been propelled up. I couldn't quite see over the top, but I could see the sun shining brightly on the other side. It was warm and beautiful there. The valley behind me was in shadow, and darkness ran all the way down the hill. Down in that dim valley was my whole life – everything I knew and believed and had experienced up to that point. I felt I wanted to step over the ridge into the warmth of the light, but feared that doing so meant that the life behind me would be gone forever. There would be no way back.

I think, in retrospect, I needed time to let the old Dave go, to grieve for him, before I could move on with my new life, with the new me. Grief can be hard to let go of.

The video we watched that night (another C-word here) talked of how you gave yourself to Jesus, what words you might use to do so, and the process involved. It all seemed straightforward and obvious, really. One term I learned of was the Prayer of Commitment, the one spoken when you give yourself to Jesus.

I spoke to Kate:

> Me, 10:49pm: "… I'm currently researching the Prayer of Commitment, and then I'm gonna do some writing."

Kate and I chatted at length that night.

> Kate: "I remember you being right on the edge, and I wished I was there for you because I could feel you were ready to surrender, but not wanting to do it alone. I know I encouraged you to talk to Jan, Annemieke and Michele the next day, because I knew they were discerning and would come to the same conclusion."

I did some writing that night, but went to bed early, as I wanted to attend Carpet Time in the morning.

And what a morning it turned out to be.

CHAPTER 13

ACCEPTING THE OFFER

Thursday 23 September 2021

Carpet Time was something I really looked forward to. It was an opportunity to meet up with some truly lovely people, eat some delicious home-made cake, listen to some really uplifting music, and to learn something about the Bible, God, or myself. Oasis Trails ran a session every day of the week, but, as much as I would have loved to have gone daily, it was a one-hour return trip, and I hated to leave my dogs at home so early. It was especially important for me to burn off some of the puppy's energy, as she was prone to eating my sofa if I left her in the house without a proper physical workout in the morning.

These worship sessions also recharged me, or rather, recharged the Spirit that I felt had taken up residence inside of me. He would always surge at these sessions, and I would always drive home elated.

Annemieke led the session on this day, opening with prayer. The Spirit always reacted strongly to her prayers, just as He did on this day. She followed prayer by reading a passage from the Bible. I opened up my new Bible app, and, despite fumbling with it, located the passage she was reading and read along with her.

Then she put on some music videos, and I sat and listened. I rarely sang along, as I hated my singing voice, and I was sure that everybody else would too. Kate always told me that God would just love it.

I was getting to know many of the songs, as they were often played at the various events that I was now frequenting. I was picking up the lyrics of the more popular ones, and many of these songs brought out powerful emotions in me. Many times, whilst listening, I would quietly wipe a tear off my cheek. It was just a kind of sublime joy I felt as the Spirit reacted to the words. I also enjoyed seeing how others sang along, or just threw themselves into worship in apparent wild abandon.

And then Annemieke played another video: *Alive in You* by *Jesus Culture* – a song I had heard a few times before. However, what made this choice of music so impactful for me was not so much the lyrics, although it does sing of 'Christ who lives within me', but the imagery used on that morning's particular video. Of the many video versions available on *YouTube*, the one Annemieke played that day had been recorded from flying drone footage – it showed two people standing at the top of a really high summit, with the sun shining on the other side of the mountain, just as I had described at last night's Alpha course.

I saw myself standing on that peak, with the glorious sun on the other side of the mountain, pulling me, beckoning me.

Tears rolled down my cheeks.

The next song was one that I'd never heard before: *Come to the Table*[15] by *Sidewalk Prophets*.

As I followed the words on the screen, a great sense of emotion surged up in me. The lyrics were basically telling *my* story. The song listed everything I had been at some time in my life – *everything*.

The music starts off slowly with a sad tone, but the tempo begins to build, as hope is clearly available for those who want it – all you have to do is just accept the simple invitation.

> *We all start on the outside*
> *The outside looking in*
> *This is where grace begins*
> *We were hungry we were thirsty*
> *With nothing left to give*
> *Oh the shape that we were in*
> *Just when all hope seemed lost*

Love opened the door for us
He said, come to the table
Come join the sinners who have been redeemed
Take your place beside the Saviour
Sit down and be set free
Come to the table
Come meet this motley crew of misfits
These liars and these thieves
There's no one unwelcome here
And that sin and shame that you brought with you
You can leave it at the door
And let mercy draw you near
So, come to the table
Come join the sinners who have been redeemed
Take your place beside the Saviour
Sit down and be set free
Come to the table
Come to the table
To the thief and to the doubter
To the hero and the coward
To the prisoner and the soldier
To the young and to the older
All who hunger all who thirst
All the last and all the first
All the paupers and the princes
All who fail, you've been forgiven
All who dream and all who suffer
All who loved and lost another
All the chained and all the free
All who follow, all who lead
Anyone who's been let down
All the lost, you have been found
All who have been labeled right or wrong
To everyone who hears this song

Oh
Come to the table
Come join the sinners, you have been redeemed
Take your place beside the Savior
Sit down and be set free
Oh
Sit down and be set free
Come to the table
Come to the table
Sit down and be set free
Come to the table.

I was being offered the opportunity to come and sit beside the Saviour at His table, a table that was full of all the misfits and losers in life, the ones He said He wanted to find and rescue.

> *"On hearing this, Jesus said, "It is not the healthy who need a doctor, but the sick."* – Matthew 9:12

I felt that the misfits and losers at the table were actually better – *stronger* – than me, because they had taken the courageous step of going up and sitting at the table, whilst I was still incapable of doing that, for whatever reason. It all seemed so simple: come and sit down at the table, and everything will fall into place.

The tempo built as the answer was becoming more obvious, and the singer was constantly beckoning me to "sit down and be set free". The Lord beckons everybody to do the same, regardless of who you are.

"*... be set free...*"

The last part of the song feels full of love, joy, and peace, and a closer look at the lyrics tells you why – the word *who* has been change to *you*: *Come join the sinners, **you** have been redeemed.*

My story started when I was invited to Wes and Sherry's table in January. I subsequently fled Ben's table in June, when he spoke of Jesus. There was always a seat for me at the table of amazing food and wonderful company at the lunch each Wednesday. The love and peace of that community always beckoned me.

I had just one more table to sit at – the most important table that ever existed – and I had an invitation to it, as indeed we all do. Do I flee this one too?

Tears were streaming down my cheeks as I sat in a chair, in the corner of the room, by the door. I wanted to get up and run, but I couldn't move.

"… *be set free…*"

The two birds…

By the time the song finished, something had changed inside of me. My mind was a whirl, my emotions surging.

As the session ended, I left the room first, headed straight to the dining room, and closed the door behind me. Shortly afterwards, Jan joined me, fully aware of my state.

He immediately hugged me, asking if I was okay.

"Wow!" he said. "Your heart is really racing. Do you wanna go for a walk or something to settle down a bit?"

My heart *was* in overdrive.

"I just wanna – I dunno – come back down…" I mumbled. I couldn't put it into words what I wanted – all I knew was that I was in a very unfamiliar place and was quite frightened.

I sat down, and he plopped himself next to me. We spoke about my situation, what had been happening, the two videos and the impact they'd had on me.

His wife, Annemieke, joined us and sat down.

We spoke about my feelings, and I told them about how I felt I was at the top of the mountain, with just one more tiny step to take.

"So, what are you waiting for?"

I couldn't give an answer. *What was I waiting for?* I knew what came next, but it felt like an admission of failure somehow, in that my life had all been completely wrong.

I knew if it didn't happen today, they'd be more C-words and weird events happening around me, until I finally accepted the truth.

The sandcastle that I had constructed, with its protective wall and keep, was continually being knocked down by the constant waves of events, ceaselessly forcing their way through everything I had done to protect myself from the relentless barrage of the past three months.

The last two waves had just surged into the remnants of what was left of those walls, and all that was visible of my defences now were just a few slight lumps, barely noticeable in the sand. My original foundations were laid bare, waiting to be rebuilt upon, just like any other destroyed defensive structure.

I had nothing more to give.

I had no reserves left to shore up my defences.

I was overwhelmed, completely finished.

I surrender.

"I'll go first, if you want?" said Jan. "Just follow me…"

He dropped to his knees on the floor in front of me.

I briefly thought of church last Sunday, when he had asked me to read a verse out from the Bible in front of everybody, and I'd made excuses not to. I felt like I'd let him down, as I'd blustered and excused myself – "No glasses," I'd explained.

I fell to my knees next to him, and Annemieke did the same.

I really had no idea what I was doing, so I bumbled through as I prayed aloud – there were no rules, I just had to be genuine, and speak from the heart.

I apologised to Jesus for my stubbornness to Him, for taking so long to get to this point. I asked Him to forgive me for all the bad things I had done in my life, of which there were many. He knew everything that was in my soul, so I didn't need to specify. I asked Him to love me as I was and invited Him to come into my heart.

When I'd finished speaking, Jan and Annemieke took their time to pray over me. The pain in my poor old knees was intruding, as I was kneeling upright on a hard wooden floor for quite some time.

When we were done, they both embraced me and welcomed me into the family as a brother.

Michele – who must have been hovering just outside of the door – came in. She didn't need telling what had just happened – her face was

Jan, me, and Michele, minutes after I accepted Jesus into my heart

beaming as she hugged me and welcomed me into God's family.

Jan grabbed his phone and took a picture of the three of us. The shiny faces are clear for all to see!

Jan quickly circulated this photo on *WhatsApp* for the wider community to know, along with this simple message:

> *Jan, 1.54pm: "Dave spoke to God. He wants, and received, Jesus as king and saviour..."*

Kate had only left Spain a day earlier for Germany, and I really wanted to be the first to tell her, so I sent her a quick message:

> *Me, 1.59pm: "I just got down on my knees with Annemieke and Jan, and invited Jesus into my heart. X."*

I felt bad that it happened after Kate had left the country, but I had always told her that if I ever did this, it would be for me and for no other reason or person. It was a deeply personal decision, and it had to be the right one for me, and me alone. Of course, I would have loved for her to be there when it happened, but it wasn't to be.

Kate was in the middle of filming when she read the message. She immediately called a halt, and celebrated my acceptance of Jesus with the people she was with, and then they prayed for me.

She responded:

Kate, 2.46pm: "Praise God!!!... I'm so happy!... I'm crying... seriously so happy!"

I cheekily replied.

"Hope I didn't spoil your meeting?"

I hadn't, of course. I could have called her up at 4.00am to tell her the news, and she would have been elated and responded likewise.

Kate: "My heart was so full of joy I couldn't stay quiet. There is nothing more important than celebrating a lost sheep found by the shepherd, and so we stopped filming and all of us rejoiced together. Tears stream down my face even now, thinking about it. I'm so grateful that God used me along your path, and while I would have been so happy to have been there and hug you in that moment, I was actually happy that I wasn't there because it's not about me – it's about Jesus, and no-one could say you were doing this because of me. This was fully your decision, and I'm so proud of you."

I stayed for lunch with the family of Jan and Annemieke before heading back to my car. As I reached it, I saw a pilgrim knocking on the door of the local *albergue*. She was clearly not getting an answer, so I had to see if I could help her.

Irene, from Germany, said she had taken the wrong fork on the *camino* just before the village and had ended up in the wrong place. She had hoped to be in *Villamayor*, a few kilometres away. I wanted to visit the staff there at the Oasis Trails *albergue* anyway, to celebrate the good news with them, so I offered to take her over with me.

It only took a few minutes to get there. As she was being checked into the place, the staff were hugging me and welcoming me to the family. We were all brothers and sisters, under one Father.

I drove back to my home village and parked up in the carpark. I wanted to go directly to the Oasis to see Wes and Sherry as well, but I bumped into Wes in the carpark, and we walked up together. They'd been out on the *camino* all day, giving out free water to thirsty pilgrims when they had received the earlier message from Jan.

Wes and I took another beaming photo, this time of the two of us together in the café.

How the Canadians must have been feeling is difficult to comprehend. Remember what Wes had written in his journal, nine months ago, back in January, at the beginning of this story?

> *Wes, 29 January 2020: "Father, thank You for the opportunity we had to listen to Dave. **I pray he will find You** in the midst of this grief. Lord, I pray for more opportunities to be able to share with Dave."*

At 7.00pm I went home. I went to my Twitter profile and made one tiny change. For years, it had simply said 'Englishman, lost in Spain'. I changed it to 'Englishman, found in Spain'.

I then called Kate.

> *Kate: "There was a lot of crying and happiness on my part during the call. I don't think a lot was said, other than you recounting the day to me, and me being filled with joy (and tears)."*

I went up to the café later and met up with Ed, Wes, and Sherry. A local couple were in, and had become friends with us all. They didn't speak a word of English though, and, in our excitement, we all chatted about the day in English, unfortunately leaving them out of the picture.

The lady asked me if I had lost weight recently, as she thought I looked quite different. I told her I hadn't. She stared at me, confused. She reached up and touched my face gently, saying, "But you *have* changed.

There's something very different about you. What's changed?"

She could see an obvious difference in me since she'd last spoken to me a few days earlier. It could only have been the shining face that had caught her attention, as she didn't know until some weeks later what had happened to me that day.

That evening, whilst out having a celebratory drink with Ed, my phone beeped constantly. I was receiving messages from people all over the world who, having heard the news, wanted to welcome me to the family. These were people I'd met coming through over the summer, either on the *camino*, at the *albergues*, the monastery, or in our local village. It was truly amazing how many people had come into my life these past few months.

What happened this day was truly monumental. In fact, many would say it was a miracle. From the staunch atheist that I was, to getting down on my knees – it was absolutely remarkable by any standards, and to do so in such a short period…

I don't know what God wanted with this atheist, but He clearly knew how to get my attention, and He knew just what it would take to get me to accept Him.

In retrospect, I think the main issue for my final stubbornness was giving up on the old me. I think I needed time to accept that the old Dave was done for. The man I had known all of my life was about to die and be reborn as something else. I needed time to mourn him.

I'm just sorry it took so long to give in to the inevitable.

PAGE 146
[15] 'Come to the Table' by Sidewalk Prophets.
Songwriters: Ben McDonald, Dave Frey, Ben Glover.
Produced by Seth Mosley and Mike O'Connor for Full Circle Music.
© 2017 World Entertainment LLC, a Curb company.

CHAPTER 14

NEW DAY

Friday 24 September 2021

I woke up feeling totally invigorated. I sent a brief message to the guys on the Alpha course group chat, and to Kate:

> *"Just did something I've never done before! I woke up as a Christian for the first time ever!"*

The only thing I needed to do next was to decide on when to be baptised. My parents had baptised me as a baby – or *christened* me – into the Church of England. As an atheist, it was something that had irritated me all of my life. I didn't think it was right to baptise children who had no say in the matter, but I understand now that raising a child in the faith is not something to worry about, as that child can make an informed decision to continue or not, once of age.

My original christening had always meant *nothing* to me, and now my pending baptism meant *everything* to me.

I couldn't wait, although I really wanted Kate to be there with me. More than anybody, I really wanted her to baptise me, for so many reasons. (You don't need to be a priest or some other 'authority' – any Christian can baptise another.) I could have waited for Kate to come back, but I just had an overwhelming desire to walk into a river and take the next step, and as soon as possible.

I suggested to Jan that we could do it at church on Sunday, and he set the wheels in motion for me. I was told to prepare a testimony that I'd have to read out on the day. To help me understand what things to think of, and what would happen on the day, I was sent three videos of baptisms the community had performed over the course of the year. They did them in a river near the city of *Estella*, where they occasionally held church.

Kate was extremely busy with interviews and filming in Germany. At 5.00pm she discovered that my baptism was to be this Sunday. I could tell from her response how sad she was at not being there.

> Me: "I just wish you could be there with me."
>
> Kate: "I wish I could too."
>
> Me: "You'd definitely be doing the dunking. First on my list…"
>
> Kate: "If I hadn't JUST left…" 😂
>
> Me: "But I know you'll be there with me. I'll feel your presence…"

Kate was working the rest of the day until late at night, so she asked to chat with me tomorrow.

In the evening, we all headed over to *Logroño* for a night out to say goodbye to one of the other volunteers at the café.

Saturday 25 September 2021

I booked a flight back to the UK to see my family, which would be the first visit back since the funeral. The trip would also coincide with Kate being in the UK – just up the road from my home town, so we agreed to meet up and visit my family together, and I promised to show her around the beautiful Cotswolds region in England, an area I'd always wanted to see.

I spent most of the afternoon and evening in the café chatting. I knew I had to go home and prepare my testimony for the baptism tomorrow, but the Oasis was full of really interesting pilgrims, and it was difficult to extricate myself.

Eventually, around about 10.00pm, I tried to leave, announcing my departure. As I reached the door, a middle-aged lady, who had been quietly sitting in the café, called to me.

"Oh, David. I was hoping to share my story with you before you left."

I really wanted – and needed – to go home, but I couldn't refuse her. I sat down and hoped it would be quick.

Her name was Becky, and she had a rather bold tattoo of a large green tree on her left upper arm. She told me of a visit to the hills near her home five years ago, in the US, with her two young daughters and a friend in the car, when a huge, snow-laden, Douglas Fir tree fell and squashed her car.

She took the brunt of the fall, and her injuries were so bad that she should've died at the scene. She suffered nineteen broken bones and spent two weeks in intensive care. Her right hand was barely attached to her arm via a muscle, her other arm and one leg also being massively damaged. She was in a coma for a while and eventually had to learn how to walk all over again.

It was only then that I noticed her arms were covered in scar tissue, and the image of the tree – the same tree that fell on her – was tattooed directly onto the extensive scar tissue.

She told me the memento was to declare that the tree had not won that day.

And now she was walking the *Camino de Santiago* – all eight hundred kilometres of it! Hers was an incredible story, and one that moved me to tears.

Wes, who had been working behind the counter whilst she was telling me her story, overheard her and approached Becky.

"I met your husband," he told her.

It transpired that she and her husband had walked part of the *camino* two years after the accident (from *Sarria* to *Santiago*). The following year, with Becky healed enough not to need her husband's support, and her husband in dire need of some space, he came to Spain and walked the whole of the *camino*. Whilst on this walk, he stopped in at the Oasis and talked with Wes. Neither he nor Becky had mentioned the Oasis café, so it was pure chance that Becky had stopped at the same place.

It was a very emotional moment, and, before Becky left, Wes and I prayed over her for healing, and for strength to finish the pilgrimage (which she did, a week early).

At 10.30pm, I was home when Kate sent me a message asking me if I'd done my testimony, which obviously I hadn't. I said I was "working on it". She was rather annoyed with me for this, as the baptism was tomorrow. We hadn't really been able to speak much all day because of her work commitments in Germany.

I suggested we chat at that moment, but Kate didn't want to interrupt me, as I was working on my testimony. I really needed help, so I pushed her.

"Your voice and wisdom might also calm my beating heart somewhat…"

"Well," she replied. "I'm available, but don't use me as an excuse to not do your work."

"I'm the only excuse I need to not do my work."

We video-chatted, and she advised me of what to say tomorrow. After we finished, I wrote out my testimony, and practised it a few times.

Sunday 26 September 2021

When I was completely happy with my testimony, it was the early hours of Sunday morning. I sent a quick message to Kate before going to bed:

Me, 1.04am: "Please know that if I had to choose just two people to walk into that river with me, it'd be Jesus and you. You mean that much to me."

In the morning, Kate responded:

Kate, 9.05am: "I know. Wish I could be there for you. But I'm thinking about you and praying for you."

Me: "I know. I will carry you in my heart into that freezing water, and your love will help to keep me warm, and your prayers will be heard by the Lord. X."

Sadly, Nath also had a prior commitment. She was away at the beach for the weekend, much to her regret. I would have loved to have had her there too. I could have considered a later date for the baptism, just to have these two amazing people there with me, but I needed to do it, and soon.

Sunday 10.30am

Ed came with me in my car, and Wes and Sherry went in theirs. For me, it felt like the morning of my wedding day – exciting, but weirdly frightening too.

We all met up in an isolated lay-by, just outside of *Estella, Navarra*. As we pulled up, several vehicles were already there, with people unloading various items of picnic furniture and pots of steaming hot food. Everybody knew the drill, as they had held church on the riverbank many times.

I got out of the car and called out to everybody, saying how lovely it was to see "all you wonderful, beaming people here!"

Annemieke instantly replied, "Welcome to the Shiny Club, Dave!"

We had to carry the various rugs and blankets, tables, food boxes, the music system, etc. down a track off the lay-by, and across the river, carefully fording our way over the slippery rocks, with the ice-cold water rushing around our shins. The younger members held the hands of the less-abled and elderly, to ensure we all got across safely.

On the other side was a clearing, and the tables were quickly set up, and coffee and tea brewed with military precision. Cakes were handed out and conversations begun. We were far out in the countryside, and I guessed we'd have poor or intermittent phone reception. It was a good thing, as ringing mobiles often interrupt emotional situations. I switched my phone off to concentrate on the here and now, although I ached at the thought of not being able to receive a message of support from Kate.

However, I knew she was with me.

Setting up: Church by the river for my baptism

After about thirty minutes of beautiful conversation, the rugs were set out and chairs and stools placed in a circle around them. It was time for the service to begin.

Jan introduced proceedings with a prayer, as usual. A few songs that meant something to me, including *Come to the Table*, followed this. Everybody joined in, singing to the Lord.

I still didn't feel comfortable about singing in a group, even though most of those guys couldn't hold a note either. As Jan said in the intro to the day (probably aimed at me): "It isn't about being able to sing well, it is about singing to rejoice. Only He listens to you, and, to Him, you sing beautifully."

Michele gave a lesson from the Bible, and, as always, did so in such a way as to be very impactful. She can make the abstract seem obvious. She connects messages from across the universe and gives clarity to the word of God.

Ed was sitting next to me, and I felt a change in him as she taught the lesson. Later, when we got back in the car, his first words to me were: "Michele was amazing. I was wrong about her. I'm seriously changing my opinion here."

The service was, of course, all directed at me. Everything in the Bible, every song played, was – and always is – directed at me, or so it seemed. But then, everybody feels that way at every service – God talks to us all individually.

Following another song, it was my turn to speak.

I'm very comfortable with public speaking; it really doesn't faze me. I have had a lot of experience from running huge international summer courses during many summers in the UK. After spending an entire morning talking to a fresh course of three hundred international students, chatting to this small group of loving family members was a walk in the park, although I would, on this occasion, actually be addressing *God*. Oh yeah, I forgot that bit – I just needed to focus on my new family, and it would all be okay.

When I wrote the speech for the tribute at Paul's funeral, it took me ages because every time I wrote an idea down, I broke down in tears. Every time I read the lines I'd written, I broke down in tears. All week I was adding to it, and all week I was in tears. I really had to practise speaking the tribute aloud, and I just could not get to the end. But on the actual day of the funeral, I focused on my delivery, and I got through it without faltering (well, I wavered slightly, once).

I had written my testimony the night before. I had been late getting home because of some powerful stories told to me by pilgrims in the café. Kate had already firmly advised me to get my act together: "This is a momentous occasion – not something you can just play by ear!"

It had only taken me about forty-five minutes to write it down, but I had to speak it through several times to make sure it sounded okay. I choked up a few times, but I got to the end, so I knew I'd be okay with it at the ceremony.

I knew from crossing the river earlier that the water was actually freezing cold, and the videos I'd seen of previous baptisms carried out here showed the speeches being made *in* the water. Those baptisms had been done in the summer, so it would have been okay then. I was worried about the cold water affecting my delivery, so when Jan suggested I do it in the circle on dry land, I was very relieved. Jan was going to perform the baptism, along with Wes, and I knew they were probably worried about the cold too.

"That's probably a good thing," I replied, "as my speech is about *thirty* minutes long, if that's okay?" Jan thought I was being serious.

This was my testimony:

> "Lord Jesus Christ, for 55 years, 9 months, and 21 days, more or less, I lived a life of complete ignorance. I thought I was happy, but I always felt that something was missing from my life. I just didn't know what it was. And I did many bad things, all of which I am deeply ashamed of.
>
> And then I met some of Your children, many of them gathered here today – The Shiny Club. And they loved me without question, and I instantly fell in love with them in return.
>
> Some of them told me about You, but I would flee the table at the first mention of Your name. I was not the right man for You, Father, or so I thought. But You had other ideas, my Lord, and You silently filled me with the Holy Spirit. Your love for me – this awful sinner – grew stronger and stronger inside of me, with each passing day.
>
> Foolishly, I tried to resist You, to question You, to challenge You, but You just loved me back harder, again and again. And again. Your hugs of me were crushing in their intensity. I just didn't understand why You wanted me so badly. I asked You repeatedly, "What do You want of me?"
>
> And then I realised. I was actually talking to You. You were real. I was talking to God. I was actually talking to You, my Father. Father, I'd like to apologise for not being there for You for the last 55 years, even though You were always there for me, patiently waiting and watching. I'm also sorry I resisted You so much these last few months.

Father, I no longer flee the table at the mention of Your name, because Your name is now written in my heart, and in my soul. I feel You inside of me. I feel You improving me, guiding me, teaching me, loving me, and forgiving me. And it is beautiful, unlike anything I could have imagined.

Lord, it is with great honour and pride that I accept Your invitation to sit at Your table with You. I open my heart to You; I dedicate my life to You; and I promise to do whatever You command me to do. I will never let You down again. Jesus, Father, please accept me into Your family, into Your Glorious Kingdom, and let me serve You faithfully from this moment forward.

I love You, Father, and I thank You."

Once complete, it was time for the immersion. The three of us waded into the water to waist height – it was freezing, but I was extremely eager. We turned and faced the gathering on the riverbank. Wes was holding my left arm, and Jan my right.

Then Jan spoke:

"Father, Father, I thank You for this moment. I thank You for the testimony of where Dave stands. You know what is behind, and You know the light that You are, and he has seen the door, You are the door, and he wants to come into Your Kingdom. He wants to say that what is behind is gone, and I want him to step into You, believing that Your Spirit will make him completely new, will renew him, a new life. So Dave, on the testimony of your own words, of your own faith, it is an honour to baptise you, in the name of the Father, in the name of the Son, and in the name of the Holy Spirit, in the name of Jesus…"

And they dipped me backwards into the freezing water, and it didn't feel cold at all. It felt amazing! I was so charged and energised that I burst up out of the water, fists blasting upwards like a goal-scorer in a World Cup match, which caught Wes and Jan completely by surprise. I was alive!

An enormous cheer went up from the gathering, with lots of clapping and laughter. One of my flip-flops got caught in the thick mud at the bottom of the river and came off, but, fortunately, floated to the surface.

As I exited the water, dripping wet, carrying my flip-flop, people came forward for a big hug, despite the discomfort of my wet t-shirt pressed against them. Once the hugs were complete, they formed a circle around me, laid hands on me, and prayed over me. I stood there, a yellow towel draped around my wet shoulders, head bowed, as they prayed.

I was lost in the moment – the power of the communal prayer was so great, I could feel an energy within me unlike anything I had ever felt before.

It was such a powerful, beautiful moment. There was just one thing missing.

And then, out of the blue, a ringing intruded on the moment. Somebody had obviously forgotten to switch their mobile off. It was very distracting, and I was annoyed, but I ignored it as best I could, and just focused on the moment.

Then I heard Annemieke walking away from the group, whilst talking to somebody. I was shocked that she would be the one on the phone at such a time as this – it was so unlike her. I assumed it must have been really urgent for her to take the call then. I asked myself which of her children were here with us, and which weren't.

I opened my eyes and glanced up. It took me a few seconds to focus and realise what it was, and even longer to understand why it was there. There was a mobile phone right in front of my face. I stared at it for a few seconds, not comprehending, then looked up at Annemieke who was holding it, my face a question.

She was just smiling back at me, and then it hit me.

"*Kate?*"

She nodded, her beautiful smile never leaving her face.

I was speechless. *She came...*

I looked straight into the camera lens and just said "Hello" with the best smile I've ever given. I couldn't see her, but I knew she was watching me over the network from Frankfurt. I was still being prayed over, so I just stared straight into the camera, straight at her, with that delirious smile of mine.

Then Annemieke turned the phone around so that I could see Kate. It looked like she was standing in the street, but I later learned she was in a café. She couldn't speak, her emotions clearly on display.

I think I said something to her, or somebody else asked something of her, I hardly recall, as I was so surprised to see my 'angel' there with me during my baptism – the one whose arrival in July had instantly lifted my spirits, the person who had always been truthful and honest, advising and guiding me in a language I could understand. Her presence there had been totally unexpected, and this was when I almost lost my composure completely.

She waved her hand in front of her face in response: *I can't speak.* Her joy at my baptism, and the fact she was absent from it, was reducing her to tears, in a café, in Frankfurt.

I couldn't speak either. I knew if I tried to speak, it'd come out in a blub, so I just smiled at her as she looked at me, neither of us doing anything more than just about managing to hold it all together.

> Kate: *"It brings me to tears even now. I wanted to be there so badly, but couldn't leave work and fly back so quickly. I was out filming that morning and rushed to find a café with wi-fi so I could be there. It took a couple of attempts calling to get through, but finally we connected. The poor waitress probably thought I was mad. With tears streaming down my face, I ordered a coffee just so that she'd let me stay. I sat there and cried the whole time, with people just staring at me as they passed by. Annemieke asked me if I wanted to pray, but I couldn't speak out loud, but prayers flowed from me like my tears. God was used to hearing my prayers for you, but I know He rejoiced with me, as my prayers had shifted a few days prior from desperate prayers for help to joyful praises of thanksgiving."*

After the prayers were over, hot food and drinks were served up, whilst Ed stripped down to his shorts, and joined me for a laugh in the river, along with some children present. This time, the water felt really cold!

I got home at 2.30pm, and shortly afterwards received *the* photo of the whole day. A volunteer from the *albergue* had taken it, and she photographed me just as I burst out of the river, clearly catching Jan and Wes by surprise!

Dave, bursting out of the water during his baptism.
(Jan, Dave, and Wes.)
Copyright © 2021 Tanisha Rae Grisel

CHAPTER 15

NEW PERSON

Sunday 26 September 2021, PM

When I arrived home, I was so tired that I took a siesta on the sofa for a few hours. When I woke up, one of my dogs was sitting on the floor next to the sofa, just staring at me. Even when I opened my eyes, she didn't flinch. It was as if she was watching something, and it was holding her attention. Since my baptism, I often turn around to find her just sitting there, staring at me without moving. It would be quite spooky if I didn't know why she was doing it. She is a very sensitive dog, and she sensed a change in me from that day, and she senses the Holy Spirit within me.

Michele always made videos of the baptisms they had. I'd seen a few of the videos prior to my baptism, and now she was at home, busily putting together the video of mine.

At 11.00pm, Michele sent me the video, but I couldn't open it. I didn't know if it was a problem with my internet or not, but nothing seemed to make a difference. Whilst I was looking to see what the problem was, Kate sent me a message: "They sent me the video. Absolutely wonderful!"

I then began receiving messages from other friends, all of whom had been sent the video, had viewed it, and loved it. I seemed to be the only one who couldn't view it!

At 11.30pm, I received a copy from Kate and watched it.

Me: "That video brought me to tears."

Kate: "Yeah, me too."

You can watch the video, just five minutes long, on *YouTube*, by following this link: https://bit.ly/3nu43Ww.

Monday 27 September 2021

Me, 11.23am: "Wow, very emotional today. Just playing frisbee with the dogs... listening to my collection of three worship songs, tears streaming down my cheeks..! I feel saved, I feel free, I feel home..."

Kate asked me if I would record a testimonial video for her church back in Alabama, as she had asked the congregation to pray for me over the past few months. It was only now that I discovered just how many prayers were being said for me, all over the world, via the extensive network of all the Christian friends that had come into my life recently.

I gladly agreed and asked her to send me the name of the church so I could look it up online to see who I would be talking to. She laughed at me, saying it was such a tiny church in the middle of nowhere, so I probably wouldn't find it.

Before long, I was finding pictures of Kate at various events at the church, so I sent her some photos to prove it was online, and to show her some old memories. After sending several pictures, Kate responded.

Kate: "Why are you being a stalker?"

Me: "The new me is limited to fifteen minutes stalking per day, and I've reached my limit."

That comment made her laugh out loud. The 'new me' was a very new me indeed. I still had my sense of humour, and I hadn't lost sight of who I was. Over the coming days and weeks, I just became a much better and happier version of myself. I had no input in that process – it was the Spirit within me, changing me. I just felt the effects of those changes, and others noticed them too.

My messages to Kate stated I felt "on fire", and I was "urging to get going". I turned to Kate for advice about what to do next.

Thursday 30 September 2021

Me: "I want to spend time with Jesus, and build a relationship with Him."

Kate: "This is easy advice - yes, do that." 😄

Naturally, Kate advised me about what I should do from then on.

Friday 1 October 2021

Whilst walking through the village, chatting with Nath, she laughed and said, "I really like this new, light version of you."

Nath lived with me, and had done so for a few years, and if anybody could see how I was changing, it would be her.

The word *light* rang a bell straightaway – I *was* much lighter, less stressed, and less worried about life. I can't explain why I felt that way, except because the Holy Spirit was hard at work, deep inside of me, chucking out the clutter and crap, and polishing up the good parts He found. He sure had a lot of work to do, and some days the feeling of pleasure from Him surged into a kind of ecstasy that can only be described as deeply spiritual. It even happened once whilst walking around the supermarket! I was focusing on my shopping list, when I felt the feeling growing stronger and stronger. At one point, I had to hold tightly onto the trolley. I was so glad to get the shopping done and get back home!

I asked Jan about the surges, and he replied.

"There is no overdose… it is good to be out of your mind, and in His heart."

It made absolute sense to me – my brain had been the one thing holding me back from accepting Jesus, and it was only when the heart was so over-filled with the love from Him that my brain just had to concede and let it go. Was that what the Spirit was doing to me? Numbing down my thoughts, like an anaesthetic of some kind?

I replied to Jan: "Sedate the brain, fill the heart to overflow! Love it."

I later asked Kate about it, and she told me to ask Jesus to turn it down slightly! Such ideas just stunned me. So I tried it out and asked Him to.

The next day I felt just a slight, sweet buzz throughout the whole day, with no surges.

Kate also told me to ask God what He was trying to tell me, as He clearly didn't do this sort of thing to make people feel high.

One day, I was standing in the kitchen, chatting to Nath over coffee. I had clean clothes on as I was going out, but Ziggy, my puppy, just wanted me to play with her slobber-covered frisbee. As we chatted, Ziggy repeatedly jumped up my legs, thrusting the dirty frisbee into my jeans, and I kept pushing her down whilst continuing to talk to Nath. This not only went on for a few minutes, but she was becoming more excitable and irritating, so I pushed her away and told her off.

Nath giggled at me.

"What's up?" I asked, curious about her response to my behaviour.

"It's funny now, seeing you *trying* to be angry."

My anger had disappeared completely, and I hadn't even realised until Nath said this. My recent outburst of 'anger' was comical to Nath.

Another day, she said something that really alerted me to how much I was changing. When my wife left home in December, she took with her the comprehensive collection of fridge magnets from all the trips we had taken together. The only few she left were ones I'd bought, or which were duplicated. The big double doors of the fridge-freezer had looked great, but now they seemed extremely bare, so I told Nath we'd replace them with magnets from places we went to. And we started to buy them, and Nath made one door for her magnets, and one door for mine.

One day, over coffee, she looked at the magnets and jumped up. On my door was a magnet of the character Grumpy from *Snow White*. He was scowling whilst holding a mug of coffee, with a message saying *I hate mornings!* My ex had bought it for me years ago, and it had been appropriate back then.

Nath took it from my door and put it onto hers, saying, "You're no longer grumpy, so this can't be on your door anymore..."

I recalled Kate's description of me from the first day we'd met: "Fiercely unhappy."

That was the day that my life was to undergo a rapid, unexpected, and powerful change, from that fiercely unhappy, angry, lost, and frustrated atheist, into the calm, smiley, totally at peace, follower of Jesus that I am today.

There have been other, more profound, changes as well. Until I found Jesus, I couldn't accept the loss of my brother. I used to fear dying, but now I don't. I recall the shock I felt when I asked Kate to be careful about something, and she said that she didn't fear dying. Now I understand where she was coming from.

As somebody once told me: "You can't threaten me with heaven!"

I'm far from perfect, and I still mess up frequently, and I'm definitely not a huge fan of churches; I have only ever worshipped once in a church to date – Kate's family church in Alabama when I went to visit her and her family in 2022. I still don't regard myself as religious – I just have a personal relationship with Jesus, and I can chat with Him anytime, anywhere, and without the involvement of any middleman. Just as *you* can.

I do not know why He came after *me*, but I am so excited to be living my life for Him now, whatever He has planned for me.

Thank You, Father.

The End

appendix

"In the secret place I have been shaping you. You have been kept in the shadow of My hand; a polished arrow, set apart for such a time as this. I am releasing your voice. I am displaying My splendour through you."
– Isaiah 49:2-3

This is my story, but it is His glory.

I didn't set out to find God, but, for some reason, He came looking for me. I had been depressed for a while before these events made themselves known to me, although He had clearly set plans in motion long before my depression began – probably going back to when He laid a desire in Kate's heart to come to Spain – maybe even before that?

Kate's arrival revealed a 'start' of sorts for me, as it was that very same evening when Nath and I discussed why I was suddenly feeling much better than I had been for a long time.

Within days, my depression was history, and I suddenly became inexplicably happy. It took a couple of months for me to finally accept that which I had been vocally against for the previous fifty-five years of my life.

I am still trying to understand why God wanted me, but I am so glad that He did. I have never felt more at peace, and so full of love and joy. For the first time in my life, I feel complete and whole.

Only since finding God have I been able to accept the loss of my brother. Only since finding God do I no longer fear death – I now understand that this life is just the beginning.

We are born with a yearning for God, as this is how God created us. If we choose not to accept God, we will never find the completeness we all know is missing from our lives.

Looking back over my life as an atheist, it is clear that every major decision I had taken was to try to find that *something* that we all feel is missing. I had been trying to fill the hole in my soul with an earthly, square peg, when the only thing that will fit it is the circular peg of God's wondrous presence. God yearns for us to love Him, and He truly loves us back.

If God can get me, He can get anybody. And if somebody with my history gave himself to Jesus, then it would have had to be so overwhelmingly real that I would have had no choice but to accept the Lord's offer to sit at His table beside Him. It was, and I did.

I truly hope that you find the same at-oneness that I have discovered. There can be nothing more important in your life than to accept the truth.

> *"Christianity, if false, is of no importance, and if true, of infinite importance. The only thing it cannot be is of moderate importance."*
> – C.S. Lewis, author

Meeting God

If you are ready to open your heart to Jesus and be saved, then do so as soon as you can – you simply need to invite Him in! If you still need further answers, please email me and I'll do my best to answer you, although there are far better qualified people than me out there.

To accept Jesus, might I suggest you go to a quiet place and talk to Him from your heart? God would love to hear from you, so just talk to Him. He will know if you are being genuine and truthful. Just remember, He is your Father, and He knows you better than you know yourself. Have an open and frank discussion with your Father. There are no rules to follow. Ask Him anything you want to.

Open your heart. Open the door to Jesus Christ and allow Him to come into your life. Ask Him to forgive you for all the bad things you have done. When you do this, He does what He says He'll do:

"As far as the East is from the West, so far has He removed our sins from us."   –Psalm 103: 12

Allow your creator to change you in ways you never even thought possible. Take your seat at the table and let your future begin.

Discipleship

Once you become a child of God, it is very important to be discipled by somebody experienced in this role. The purpose of discipleship is to be guided on your path as you become more like Jesus. This is not a course or a task, but a relationship of mentoring and educating. Pray that God will place the right person or people in your life for this.

Baptism

Even though you may have been baptised before, giving yourself to God (or re-giving yourself) means you want to put your past life behind you and start over again. A baptism is an outward sign of this – it shows you have received the forgiveness and cleansing of your sins through Jesus, and is a public proclamation of your belief in Jesus.

It can be done in a church, a swimming pool, a lake, or river, and it can be done by *any* Christian. For somebody who has just given themselves to Christ, it is all you desire. You become the bride on your wedding day, and you show you are a newborn child of God, that you have died to the old self. As you come out of the water, you are expressing that the old you is done, and the new you has come.

You are a born-again Christian.

A new life. A new start. A new way. Jesus' way.

"For I know the plans I have for you," declares the Lord, "plans to prosper you and not to harm you, plans to give you hope and a future. Then you will call on Me and come and pray to Me, and I will listen to you. You will seek Me, and find Me, when you seek Me with all of your heart."   – Jeremiah 29:11-13

ACKNOWLEDGEMENTS
& TESTIMONIES

I am so grateful for all that happened to me in the second half of 2021. This story couldn't have existed without the direct intervention and selfless input from the following, amazing people, all of whom deserve my utmost gratitude, deepest respect, and unending love for what they did – and continue to do – for me.

My new Christian friends (all of whom are absolutely 'normal'!) will be the first to deny any involvement in bringing me to follow Jesus, choosing instead to praise the Lord for His love and grace, as indeed do I. However, I will be eternally grateful to the Shiny Club for their role in saving me, even if they refuse to accept it!

I love you all, and I thank God for sending you to find me and giving me a place I can truly call home.

My biggest thank you, of course, has to go to my amazing friend Kate. What I did to deserve having you in my life, I know not. I cannot praise you enough, and not just for your obvious involvement in my salvation, but for your ongoing love and support in my life since that *first* day we met, not to mention the amount of selfless work you have put into helping me to complete this book. Your many proofreads, suggestions, friendly (and often brutal) feedback, and your attention to detail, have just been amazing, and so much fun.

Even that eleven-hour drive with you across four states was just so easy!

Without you, Kate, this book just wouldn't exist.

KATE LEAVELLE

"There is a pure and overwhelming joy in watching someone come to Christ and find truth and life. It is a humbling honor when you get to be part of that journey. Walking with Dave from pain to peace, from misery to joy, from loneliness to love, and to see Jesus Christ transform him from dead to alive has been one of my greatest treasures.

Watching his enthusiasm to share the Gospel with others has been another. I pray God uses him and this book to bring more people into the freedom and salvation that makes life worth living, and death the adventure that awaits."

https://www.instagram.com/thegroundedwanderer
https://www.thegroundedwanderer.net

NATHALIA CARVALHO LIMA

*"During the first half of 2021, Dave was clearly very unhappy and depressed – he was just sinking deeper and deeper.
Then one day in July he came home from the village in a much happier place, so I asked him what had happened.*

Over the next week, I watched in amazement as he went from a deep depression to a man full of laughter and fun, so much so that it was hard to comprehend it was the same person! He became much lighter, full of joy, and nothing seemed to stress him or depress him anymore. It made me so happy to see him like that.

I was really happy when he later told me he had accepted Jesus and was going to be baptised. He had always been a really nice guy, but now he is a much improved version – the kind of person you want in your life.

I cannot say what caused him to change so dramatically, apart from that which he tells me, but I witnessed an almost instant and beautiful change in him, and that is priceless."

(https://www.instagram.com/naath_carvalho_/)

WES AND SHERRY (The Canadians)

"We love watching God use His ordinary people to play a part in His ultimate plan – whether it is to pray, plant seeds, water them or take part in the harvest. It's been a joy to watch God answer those prayers that have been spoken around the world for Dave! We've seen the miracle firsthand of how Jesus has been transforming Dave's life – from atheist to acceptance – and know that He isn't finished with him yet.

Dave, we are "certain that God, who began the good work within you, will continue His work until it is finally finished on the day when Christ Jesus returns." (Philippians 1:6). All glory be to the one and only God "who wants all people to be saved and to come to a knowledge of truth." (1 Timothy 2:4).

May the truth written within these pages resonate with many – and move them to follow the One who gives life to the fullest!

ALL are welcome at the table!"

JAN AND ANNEMIEKE

"The reality of who God is, His greatness beyond comprehension, His love for those who don't love Him, His creativity – this is all again made clear in this story. It is our prayer that the plant life that started for Dave as he died as a seed, will grow strong, and reach the stage of fruit bearing.
We know it will not happen through his own capabilities, but we know that You, God, are able to do this.

May there be more to follow."

BEN VERKAAR

"This is a remarkable story about the persistent and consistent love of God for a friend of mine, who was not only against any form of traditional religion, but also strongly rejected the very idea of the existence of God. Building a wall around himself, he seemed to be unreachable and would run from the table as soon as the name of Jesus was mentioned. However, cracks in his wall started to appear when some followers of Jesus refused to give up on him. God's love can reach anywhere and anybody.

Dave tried to reject any sign that might have come from God for as long as he could until his wall came tumbling down and he surrendered his life fully to Jesus. In doing so, he transformed into a new person, clearly visible for everyone to see.

This is just the beginning for Dave."

MICHELE VANDE STEEG

"I saw a heart transform. And when a heart transforms, everything else follows. The Truth transforms us and when Dave chose to build his life on this Truth, I saw a man go from being consumed by himself and his circumstances to being consumed by the love and grace of Jesus. I saw a man set free."

(https://www.facebook.com/michele.steeg)

Gallery

The author at home during his depression months.
(March 2021)

Sherry, Nath, Dave, and Wes. (5th April)

The author on his new bike. (6th June)

The owl that came to visit. (2nd July)

Setting out on the picnic. (13th July)

Viana. (13th July)

My first Community Lunch. (14th July)

Sherry, Wes, me, and Kate at Castillo Villamayor de Monjardin.
(14th July)

Leg cramp in the lavender field.
(14th July)

Community Lunch at the Monastery, Barbarin.
(21st July)

Dave and Nath in Viana. (29th July)

Nath playing football at her first Community Lunch.
(4th August)

Dave and Kate on the camino near Viana. (3rd September)

*Kate, Rose, Andie, and Dave about to film 'Katey Eats Stuff'
on the camino. (6th September)*

*Jan and Annemieke being interviewed by Kate.
(7th September)*

Dave crossing the Pyrenees. (13th September)

Dave and Kate climbing the Pyrenees. (13th September)

Community Lunch.
(29th September)

Ed, Wes, and Dave cycling around the Basque country.

Community church in a meadow.

Friends at Dave's 55th birthday party. (5th September)

Dave and friend at his birthday party.
(5th September)

Michele and Jet praying over Nath at Dave's birthday party.
(5th September)

Andie, Rose, and Dave walking the camino.
(6th September)

Dave with Rasta and Nath at Bar Casita Lucia on the camino
near Viana, Navarra.

Rasta loving on Wes.

Still waters: baptism spot.

Praying over Dave at his baptism.

The relics of Saint Veremundo.

ABOUT THE AUTHOR

I published my first book way back in 2014, under the pen name of Diem Burden. Since then, I have published a collection of stories of my time as a front-line police officer in the UK. In 2020, I began working on my first novel, just before Covid hit us all, and changed my world.

Since finding Jesus, my priorities have changed significantly. *Come to the Table* is the story of that year, and now that this book is published, I will return to the novel I was writing before, unless God wants me to do something else.

HOW TO CONTACT THE AUTHOR

I'd love for you to sign up for my newsletter! I'll give you a free ebook as a thank you. Called *Cop Stopper*, this short memoir is a humorous look at my childhood, and perhaps why I should never have become a cop in the first place! Sign up here. http://eepurl.com/rgaDH

Follow my life on Instagram: http://www.instagram.com/Diem_Burden
My Facebook author page: http://www.facebook.com/DiemBurden
My Twitter account: http://www.twitter.com/DiemBurden
My author website: http://www.diemburden.com/
My Amazon author page: https://amzn.to/3bBrwCs

If you have any questions, comments, or feedback, I'd love to hear from you: diemburden@gmail.com

Thank you for reading my work. If you enjoyed reading this book, please consider leaving a review at the place where you bought it

Thanks again,

Diem Burden

COMING SOON

LOOK OUT FOR MY NEW BOOK:
LISTEN TO THE CAMINO

Pilgrims have been walking the *Camino de Santiago* for over 1000 years, during which time a lot of history has been made along the way, with much of it in danger of fading into oblivion.

Listen to the Camino is a book that recounts some of that lost history as you make your pilgrimage, along with tales from the present age - history is still being made each and every day!

Packed full of tips and advice for each stage of your pilgrimage, *Listen to the Camino* will make your pilgrimage more authentic and relevant.

Maximise your *camino*, listen to the *camino*.

Printed in Poland
by Amazon Fulfillment
Poland Sp. z o.o., Wrocław